Chaucer
and the
Canterbury Tales

Blackwell Introductions to Literature

This series sets out to provide concise and stimulating introductions to literary subjects. It offers books on major authors (from William Shakespeare to James Joyce), as well as key periods and movements (from Anglo-Saxon literature to the contemporary). Coverage is also afforded to such specific topics as 'Arthurian Romance'. While some of the volumes are classed as 'short' introductions (under 200 pages), others are slightly longer books (around 250 pages). All are written by outstanding scholars as texts to inspire newcomers and others: non-specialists wishing to revisit a topic, or general readers. The prospective overall aim is to ground and prepare students and readers of whatever kind in their pursuit of wider reading.

Chaucer
and the
Canterbury Tales

A Short Introduction

John C. Hirsh

Blackwell
Publishing

© 2003 by John C. Hirsh

350 Main Street, Malden 02148-5018, USA
108 Cowley Road, Oxford OX4 1JF, UK
550 Swanston Street, Carlton, Victoria 3053, Australia
Kurfürstendamm 57, 10707 Berlin, Germany

First published 2003 by Blackwell Publishers Ltd, a Blackwell Publishing company

Library of Congress Cataloging-in-Publication Data

Hirsh, John C.
    Chaucer and The Canterbury tales : a short introduction / John C. Hirsh
      p.   cm. – (Blackwell introductions to literature)
    Includes bibliographical references and index.
    ISBN 0-631-22561-7 (alk. paper) – ISBN 0-631-22562-5 (alk. paper)
    1. Chaucer, Geoffrey, d. 1400.   2. Chaucer, Geoffrey, d. 1400.
Canterbury tales.   3. Poets, English–Middle English, 1100–1500 –
Biography.   4. Christian pilgrims and pilgrimages in literature.
5. Tales, Medieval–History and criticism. I. Title. II. Series.
    PR1905 .H54 2003
    821′.1—dc21

                2001004356

A catalogue record for this title is available from the British Library.

Set in 10.5 on 13 pt Meridien
by Ace Filmsetting Ltd, Frome, Somerset
Printed and bound in Great Britain
by MPG Books Ltd, Bodmin, Cornwall

For further information on
Blackwell Publishing, visit our website:
www.blackwellpublishing.com

For
Douglas Gray

Contents

Note on Illustrations

The illustrations in this book reflect two different ways of reading the *Canterbury Tales*, one responsive to a representational, the other to a socially constructed, interpretation. The cover illustration is an extraordinarily popular early nineteenth-century painting by the British artist Thomas Stothard (1755–1834), *The Pilgrimage to Canterbury*, painted between 1806 and 1807. It is preserved in the Tate Gallery, London, and is Number 1163 in the Tate Catalogue. Stothard's painting brilliantly reflects the Romantic assumptions of his age, and, though it does not ignore the pilgrims' social roles, it is far more responsive to them as individuals, and represents in the first place their individuality and their implied relationships, and only then their relative social standing.

The illustrations within the text are William Caxton's woodcuts in the 1483 edition of the *Canterbury Tales* (*Short Title Catalogue* 5083), Caxton's first illustrated edition of the work, which he first published in 1477 (*Short Title Catalogue* 5082). They are listed in Edward Hodnett, *English Woodcuts 1480–1535*, revised edition (Oxford, 1973). They privilege the function and status of the pilgrims, and encourage a reading of the *Canterbury Tales* in which social reality is mediated rather than described, and the distinction between text and context becomes less apparent. The Caxton woodcut numbers in Hodnett are these:

The Knight	214	The Wife of Bath	227
The Squire	215	24 Pilgrims around a Table	233
The Friar	219	Troilus and Cresyde	1009
The Doctor of Physic	226		

All woodcuts © British Library, London.

Preface

This book seeks to encourage beginning students and others to read the *Canterbury Tales* with interest, knowledge and, so as not to dodge the issue, pleasure. Its focus is on the tales more than the tellers, but it seeks to respond to both, while also remaining attentive to recent developments in Chaucer studies. It is aimed at alert beginning readers who have not read Chaucer much, but who, for whatever reason, are about to do so, whether for the first time or again. I have not tried to say the last word about anything, or to write a little essay on individual tales, though that may be the office of some of my readers. If it is, I have tried to help you write a good one, whether by beginning a line of thought which may lead elsewhere, indicating an origin or a development, or simply offering a target for dissent. A select list of books relevant to Chaucer and the *Canterbury Tales* appears in the Bibliography, which is annotated. Mindful of my audience, I have kept the footnoting as light as possible, though I hope the annotated Bibliography will prove of use and interest.

My greatest debt is to the dedicatee, Professor Douglas Gray, the first J. R. R. Tolkien Professor of Middle English Language and Literature at Oxford, for many things, but primarily for keeping many of us reminded that literature in general, and medieval literature in particular, need not be regarded as an affectation of the privileged – the *Canterbury Tales* itself is witness too – but that it is still an art which both reflects and illuminates, even as it evokes pleasure and response. I am grateful to him as well for a careful and considered reading of the typescript of this book, and for useful and perceptive comments upon it. I have debts to other Chaucerians as well, to my

Preface

late father, Edward L. Hirsh, of Boston College; to the late J. Burke Severs and Albert E. Hartung of Lehigh. I record too more general gratitude to my present medieval colleagues, Sarah McNamer, Penn R. Szittya and Kelley Wickham-Crowley, who have, by example, collegiality or advice, speeded my way, but bear no responsibility for anything which follows. Charles Tung of Berkeley has kindly read parts of the volume, but he is guiltless too. Much of this book, together with certain other medieval projects, was written while I was a Keeley Visiting Fellow at Wadham College, Oxford, and I am most grateful to the Warden and to all the fellowship both for my election, and for warm cordiality while I was resident in Oxford. I am indebted as well, for good advice and good company, to Andrew McNeillie, poet, diarist, founder of the series in which the book appears, and Literature Editor at Blackwells; to Alison Dunnett, Deputy Managing Editor at Blackwells; and to Juanita Bullough, my able desk editor, for expert advice and assistance during the editorial process.

J. C. H.
Georgetown University
Washington, DC

1

Who Was Geoffrey Chaucer?

Sometime not very long before 1344, or perhaps in 1344 (the exact year is unknown), a well-connected London wine merchant called John Chaucer celebrated the birth of his first child, a son whom he named Geoffrey. John was about thirty years old, so no longer young by the standards of his time, but thanks in part to a socially advantageous marriage to Agnes, daughter of John de Copton, his years had brought a fair measure of accomplishment, respect and prosperity. Not that John Chaucer's was an old London family. His roots were in Ipswich, where Geoffrey's great-grandfather owned property, including an inn, and in a 1991 *Chaucer Review* article Lester Matheson plausibly suggested that it was probably his grandfather, Robert de Dynyngton, who both made the move to London and changed the family name to Chaucer, a word which had lost its original French association with shoemaking, and that he may have done so out of respect for a London mercer named John le Chaucer for whom he had worked, and who had left him a generous bequest in his will.

Robert Chaucer, Geoffrey's grandfather, had flourished in London as he had in Ipswich, where successful merchants were respected equally for their knowledge of their trade and for their entrepreneurial acumen, both of which could be useful to the crown. He entered the king's service in 1305, beginning an association which was concerned both with supplying wine to the royal table and overseeing the tax revenues which came from wine imports, an activity in which Geoffrey would follow him. Robert's stepson John maintained his father's courtly, and no doubt also his business, connec-

The Knight (Hodnett No. 214)

tions, including those in France and Italy. Thus, Geoffrey Chaucer was born into an able and prosperous family, one in which there was no question that, whatever else he did, when the time came for the young man to make his way in the world, he would have a well-connected and sharp-eyed family behind him.

He was also born into a London which was virtually an education in itself. It had a population of perhaps 50,000 people, at a time when only a small handful of English cities (four or five) had over 5,000. It was the center of commerce for the country as a whole, which was still largely agricultural, deeply attached to sheep-grazing, but no longer content simply to export sheep's wool to Europe: clothmaking was a growing activity. But closer to home what mattered was the court. Chaucer was born into one of the most active and flourishing parts of a city which was, in anyone's eyes, the most important in the country. He was probably born in a house on Thames

Street, in a part of the city called Vintry Ward or simply the Vintry, a block or so north of the river Thames, where other wine merchants, including some from Italy, also lived and worked. The house was not far from Old St. Paul's, and, like many London properties, was owned by a religious order to whom 60 shillings a year was due in rent, but it was altogether appropriate for his wine-merchant father, which, as Derek Pearsall has perceptively pointed out in his *Life of Geoffrey Chaucer*,[1] probably meant that it had a spacious cellar for wine, and one or more well-appointed rooms above in which business transactions could take place. It was by no means a poor man's dwelling, but neither did it isolate young Geoffrey from the life of the city as a whole.

In his excellent biography of Chaucer to which I have just referred and to which, as to the 493 direct references to his public career printed in Martin M. Crow and Clair C. Olson's *Chaucer Life-Records*,[2] I am indebted throughout this chapter, Derek Pearsall remarks that, although 30 years ago we might have found remote parts of Spain which could replicate something at least of the "atmosphere" of medieval London, today we should have to travel to Morocco to do so. In a way Pearsall is right, since some of the features of medieval London, its mixture of farmyard and city, of animals in the unpaved streets and the sound of church bells, find no convenient parallel near at hand, but for other aspects of the medieval, or at least pre-industrial, city, we need not go so far afield.

Very close to Aldgate, where Chaucer spent his most productive years, runs Whitechapel High Street, which gives into Whitechapel Road, until it becomes Mile End Road and escapes the city. But for the better part of a mile it is possible to notice, indeed it is difficult to escape, a sense of a self-contained, connected and active community, one in which self-interest mixes easily with religious precept and commercial advantage, and in which an apparently disconnected past seems somehow to account for a quick and vibrant present. Since the 1980s, the area has attached itself to the East London Mosque, built with support from Saudi Arabia, whose call to prayer seems to unify the motions of the streets, and is, in its way, as culturally powerful as any medieval church bell. A vibrant street-market operates most days, echoing in their way the many export—import "trade-only" storefronts which dot the street. Mixed in with these are the legends of the past: the 1888 "Whitechapel" or

"Jack the Ripper" murders, which for five months convulsed these streets and reminded other Londoners that there were those whose lots were hard indeed; the Royal London Hospital (as it now is) which for four years, until his death in 1890 aged just 27, was the residence of Joseph Merrick, the so-called "Elephant Man," much visited by the wealthy, by Queen Alexandra and others; even, since 1884, Toynbee Hall, built to encourage Oxford and some Cambridge students to visit the East End, and, like Chaucer's Clerk, to learn as well as to teach, so advancing continuous learning for everyone. Today Toynbee Hall, much expanded, is an active community center. This is a place whose Jewish immigrant past seems to have prepared the way for its Bangladeshi present, but it has, too, something of the medieval mix of sales on the street and imports from afar, of felt ecclesiastical presence and barely restrained commercial energy, of power quietly exercised elsewhere in the city and a parliament not quite connected to these realities, of a mix of peoples, languages, attitudes and advantages, and these are everywhere present.

Many of the children here have some knowledge of five or more languages and dialects – Seleti, Bengali, Arabic, Hindi, and English – a fact which is worth keeping in mind when reflecting upon Chaucer's knowledge of French and Italian, and though two of these they may owe to mosque school, a third to grandparents or to videos from India, they are all somehow connected to the varied, intense, and active lives they lead, filled with wonder, like the one which, in an earlier London, youngish Geoffrey Chaucer may have led, not a mile away. One other aspect of the language which these children speak has a certain relevance for one other Chaucerian debate, for the occasional or frequent mixing of languages in Whitechapel may echo, if imperfectly, the interplay of Middle English and Anglo-French forms of speech which, if scholars like W. Rothwell are not mistaken, informed, even charged, his poetry, and changed the English language forever.[3]

Probably the one thing which contributed most to the social mobility which Chaucer's family, among many others, enjoyed, was the appearance of the Black Death, the devastating plague which, transmitted by fleas on rats, first appeared in England in 1348. John Chaucer took his family to Southampton in 1348, and did not return to London until it was safe to do so, but it is interesting that, in his later poetry, Chaucer mentions the Black Death hardly at all. The appearance of the plague was unpredictable, and its effect differed greatly from place to place. Some towns and villages were devastated, others hardly touched by it. It may have brought with it, momentarily at least, an increased interest in religion, but it also seems to have contributed to the wealth of some. As often happens in times of hardship, the rich became richer. In 1349 Chaucer's mother, Agnes, inherited London shops and gardens from an uncle, Hamo de Copton, who may very possibly have died in the plague.

It was during the period of the Black Death that Chaucer's schooling, such as it was, came about, and that circumstance may help account for the fact that there seems to be virtually no record, anywhere, of when or where that education took place. It is possible that, as an only child, special efforts were made, and private tutors engaged, to keep him away from any possible contagion. There was a well-supplied Almonry School for young children at St. Paul's, minutes away from Chaucer's home, and the best guess is that he went there. He should have, but we don't really know. As he was going to make his way in court what he needed was the education of a gentleman, and, however he obtained it, that seems to be what he received. It is generally agreed that he was not attached to the Inns of Court, and, in spite of an implied interest in university life suggested by the inclusion of the Clerk among his pilgrims and by two tales set in Oxford and Cambridge, that he did not attend university. There are certainly no records preserved which suggest that he did so, and the only real difficulty in saying that his education was as limited as it seems to have been, was his love of books, which he read attentively, but with a certain system as well. He became acquainted with several encyclopedias and florilegia (collections of selections from other works), and his reading of Latin, Italian, and (especially) modern French literature was surprisingly wide. He was well read in classical literature, and in later years, as John M. Fyler has argued in *Chaucer and Ovid*,[4] owed more to Ovid than to other classical authors, using the *Metamorphoses* as a kind of mythological handbook while responding to Ovid's love poems with a mixture of deference and irony. While this sort or reading does not by itself point to a specific kind of education (indeed, the interest in modern French literature points instead to a kind of general well-roundedness unconnected to education), his reading was deep enough to suggest that one of the circles in which he moved was probably quite explicitly literary, and that some of the knowledge of which he was to give evidence was probably acquired from others who shared his interests. But perhaps not. Perhaps he was an autodidact who simply followed his own lights – and they led him into libraries. As far as Chaucer's schooling is concerned, important as the issue is, much is pure conjecture, including most of what I have written here. We really know almost nothing.

Even so, it would certainly be interesting to know when his literary interests first appeared, and whether they were in any way in conflict with his parents' apparent values, attitudes and assumptions. The record of his life, bare as it is, suggests that as a very young man, and in spite of literary interests he may have had, he did what was expected of him. When he first appears in person in Crow and Olson's *Chaucer Life-Records*, it is April 1357, and he is already in service to Elizabeth, Countess of Ulster, almost certainly as a young, teenaged page, who, according to the record, received 2 shillings and 6 pence for a short jacket, a pair of shoes, and some red and black hose. We do not know when he began his service, or in what exactly it consisted. The appointment may have been a plum, something his parents had arranged carefully. Elizabeth was the wife of Lionel, Count of Ulster, and, more importantly, second son of King Edward III. A page, if that was what Chaucer was, would normally be between 10 and 17 years of age, of a good family, and with connections. But being a page could involve hard, and rather menial, work. Apart from his sometimes interesting duties in court, a page could have been called upon to perform any of a thousand simple tasks, though he would also be taught how to behave among the nobility, and would be in regular contact with its most noble members. He also would have traveled with the household when it moved, and thus become known to, and come to know, others, at greater or lesser manor houses. But being a page was not a dead-end job. In time, as the page grew to manhood, it was understood that he would move up in the household, and that his training in arms, though elementary, might one day be of use to his lord. It may have been in Elizabeth's household that Chaucer came to understand the nature of chivalric obligation, and also the ways in which both social and human relationships were constructed. Depending upon circumstances, it is just possible that he may also have deepened his book-learning, particularly if he found a clerk, or simply a like-minded friend, who would teach him.

Two years later there is no doubt as to what Chaucer's office had become. In 1359–60, he appears at last in Lionel's retinue when the Count was campaigning in France during that interminable and destructive series of battles and conflicts known as the Hundred Years' War. Chaucer was captured at Rethel, then "Retters," near Reims, a city of real importance for the French, since it was there that they crowned their kings, and it is believed that King Edward, who then held King John of France captive, expected to be crowned King of France himself in Reims cathedral. Though the circumstances of Chaucer's capture are unrecorded, he did not remain a prisoner for very long, and there is a record that King Edward himself contributed £16 to his ransom.

It was probably during the 1360s that Chaucer, a smart and able young man in his twenties, began to write poetry. This was a period of relative stability and order in England, the result, at least in part, of a 1360 peace treaty with France, which was to last until 1369. In 1366 he undertook a journey to Navarre, for unknown purposes: pilgrimage to St. James of Compostella is possible, though court business more probable, possibly in connection with plans which Edward, the Black Prince, was entertaining. Two years later, in 1368 he again traveled abroad – this time certainly on court business, though his destination is uncertain – as he did on the following year. No less important to him was his meeting and eventual marriage to Philippa de Roet, lady of the queen's household and the oldest daughter of the Flemish knight Sir Paon de Roet, and, in spite of a recent challenge to this identification by H. A. Kelly,[5] very probably the sister of Katherine, known to history as Katherine Swynford. Soon after their marriage, in 1367, Philippa gave birth to a son who was named Thomas, the poet's first offspring, born about a year after John Chaucer's death. The boy would grow up to become a courtier and public servant of some distinction, like his father, who in the 1360s had begun traveling on the king's behalf, including one trip in 1368 which seems to have lasted more than one hundred days, and may have taken him at least to Milan, and possibly further.

But there were other and more powerful forces at work. About 1370, shortly after the death of his first wife Blanche, Duchess of Lancaster, John of Gaunt, the powerful third son of King Edward III

(d. 1377) and uncle of King Richard II, drew Chaucer into his ever-increasing orbit. John of Gaunt was Earl of Richmond and later Duke of Lancaster, and in about 1370 he took Katherine Swynford as his mistress, an action which led to an immediate upward adjustment in the fortunes of Katherine and all who were associated with her. In the next year, however, John of Gaunt married Constanza of Castile, daughter of Pedro of Castile, sealing what seemed to be an important alliance for England, and opening the possibility, never realized, of a Spanish crown for John himself. It was not until 1394, after 23 years of marriage, that Constanza (her English name would have been Constance, which Chaucer uses in the *Man of Law's Tale*) died, so that in 1396 John of Gaunt was at last free to marry Katherine Swynford, very probably the sister of Chaucer's wife, by whom the great Duke had four children. He himself died in 1399, a year before Chaucer and King Richard II.

The date of Chaucer's earliest work is almost entirely conjectural. We know that by the late 1360s he was engaged in writing *The Book of the Duchess*, a dream-vision elegy, among other things, about Blanche, Duchess of Lancaster, John of Gaunt's first wife, who had died in 1367, and he would have been unlikely to have undertaken this project except that he had already begun to become known as a writer. It was almost certainly earlier in this decade that he undertook his translations of the *Roman de la Rose*, an allegorical French love poem begun by Guillaume de Lorris (dates uncertain) in the first half of the thirteenth century, and continued after 1275 by Jean de Meung (d. *c*.1305). About this time he also wrote lyrics in English and French, though it is impossible to say whether he was or was not the author of some fairly mediocre French poems from *about* this date signed "Ch."[6] The taste for French culture had been general in England for centuries, particularly in periods of relative peace. Not that the 1370s was a time free of war. John of Gaunt's elder brother, Edward Prince of Wales, known as Edward the Black Prince (d. 1376) spent much of the decade fighting on the Continent, most successfully in Spain and most notoriously in France, where his 1370 sack of Limoges set a new standard for brutality. Edward, Prince of Wales, was King Edward III's first son, so that his offspring, not that of his powerful younger brother John of Gaunt, was next in line for the throne. The Prince died in 1376, but not before fathering a son, Richard of Bordeaux (royal children were initially called after the place of their birth before their first official elevation), who in 1377, when King Edward III died, thus became King Richard II, though he was then only ten years old.

During the 1360s, however, when Chaucer began writing and translating poetry, King Edward III's court was particularly hospitable to the arts, and it is possible that it may even have encouraged writing and performance in English as well as in French. The dignity thus accorded English was both relatively new but also unmistakable. Of course, writing would continue in French (and also, in ecclesiastical and other circles, in Latin) throughout this period, and attorneys would continue to speak and write French (or the English version of it, Anglo-Norman) for many years to come, but for those for whom culture was not intrinsically French, English was becoming the preferred tongue.

It is probably for this reason that Chaucer not only read the *Roman de la Rose* attentively, but probably decided to translate it into English. The translation which has been attributed to him comes down to us in only three fragments, and parts of each of them are brilliant, though by themselves they might not have held the attention of posterity for very long. The translator's admiration for his text is at once apparent but grudging, and perhaps its closest connection to the later Chaucer is its attention to narrative voice, its hint of personal, if not moral, judgment, and more than either of these, its English empirical hardening of continental literary conventions. But reading it, you can see why it would have confirmed Chaucer's reputation, and why, in 1368, John of Gaunt would have permitted its author to write about his recently deceased, and much loved, wife.

In the 1370s, Chaucer, now in his thirties, had suddenly to shoulder more responsibility. War with France had begun again, and in 1369 the poet was campaigning with John of Gaunt in Picardy, where the Squire of the *Canterbury Tales* (was Chaucer thus idealizing his own youth?) also served. In 1370 he traveled abroad on the king's business, but we do not know where, or for what purpose. In 1372 he was again traveling, this time in the company of two Italian merchants who were living in London, Giovanni di Mari and Sir Jacopo di Provano, going to Italy in order to negotiate a secure port of entry for Italian goods, and also calling in at Florence, for purposes which are unclear. We do not know his return route on either this or a subsequent trip to Italy (in 1378 he was in Lombardy on diplomatic matters), and it is possible that on one of these trips he made a diversion to visit Rome, a city which would have been of the greatest interest to him and which he mentions throughout the *Canterbury Tales*. Likely though it may seem, we have yet to find hard evidence that, then or later, he yielded to the temptation to visit Rome, a city which figures prominently in many of the *Canterbury Tales*. His attitude toward the city was conflicted, and reflected its reputation both as a seat of ecclesiastical power and probity, as in the *Man of Law's Tale*, and of corruption, as in the description of the Pardoner in the *General Prologue*, whose pardons, come from Rome 'all hot', may *not* have been forgeries.

The possibilities of Chaucer's Italian journeys are even more luxuriant than the facts concerning them. It is just possible (though by no means certain) that it was on the 1378 trip to Lombardy that he secured manuscript copies of Boccaccio's works, and perhaps works of other authors like Dante. But wherever Chaucer came upon it, it may well have been Boccaccio's *Decameron* which gave him the idea to write a collection of closely connected tales founded upon a single central event. Between 1377 and 1381 he went to France and to Flanders relatively often in connection with protracted peace negotiations.

The 1370s was also a time of endings. Two of the greatest Italian authors, Petrarch and Boccaccio, both died in this decade: Petrarch in 1374, Boccaccio in 1375. As we have already seen, in June of 1376 Edward the Black Prince died, followed by his father, King Edward III, in June of the following year. The Great Schism began in 1378, leaving one pope in Rome (Urban VI, supported by the English) and one in Avignon (Clement II, supported by the French). The world of Chaucer's youth was over. A new one had begun.

But this new world had its compensations. For one thing, Chaucer's work was being recognized by the court. In 1374 he was awarded a pitcher of wine daily by the king (possibly as a reward for poetry), and an annuity of £10 by John of Gaunt. More to the point, he was in the same year appointed Controller of Customs for hides, skins, and wool in the Port of London, a most important position in a country like England for which the export of wool was such a vital matter. He kept this important office for 12 years, and his work was frequently and officially acknowledged and rewarded throughout his tenure. No wonder he was now able to rent a house in Aldgate. And then on July 12, 1376 he had a real windfall. A merchant named John of Kent had foolishly tried to evade customs duties on slightly over £71-worth of wool; he had been caught, and the value of his wool was awarded to Chaucer. The sum was more than seven times what he made in a year. Diligence had its rewards. So did connec-' tions. War or no war, it seems clear that the support he had from John of Gaunt allowed Chaucer to weather the great changes which were taking place (in 1378 those acting for young King Richard II had substituted an annuity of 20 marks for the daily pitcher of wine), and things looked at least reasonably good. His poetry was developing as well.

Again, we are not sure precisely what Chaucer was writing throughout the 1370s, but it almost certainly included some texts which he would, in the next decade, incorporate into the *Canterbury Tales*. The *Second Nun's Tale* was very probably written to celebrate the elevation of an English cardinal, Adam Easton, OSB, in December, 1381. An early version of the *Knight's Tale* dates from the final years of the 1370s, as may the beginning of the ironic, sophisticated but unfinished and finally unsatisfying work known as the *House of Fame*. This work concerns more than anything the power and place of poetry, and it is generally agreed that Chaucer must have written it after one at least of his Italian journeys, partly because of the echoes of Dante it contains, partly because of its more or less obvious attempt to come to terms with a somewhat non-English view of poetry. That coming-to-terms is most apparent in one of the poem's funniest and certainly its most famous scene: the point in the beginning of the second Book when Chaucer is picked up by an eagle, who calls him by name ("Geoffrey!"). The joke is that the poet is thus shown as being caught up into a poetic rapture, from which his vision will proceed, taking him to a place which will reveal all to him, and so transform his art. No wonder the poem is unfinished! It's one thing to say "I'm going to reveal everything about the practice of poetry," but it's quite another to do it. Chaucer gave up writing the poem just as a "man of great authority" is about to appear and revel everything – or was he? There has been much debate about who that man may have been, but Chaucer may not have known any more than we do. He simply recognized that it was time to stop writing about poetry, and, perhaps, simply to write it. But there is one other important fact about the *House of Fame*: its length. At 2,158 lines it was Chaucer's greatest effort to date, longer than the (already completed) *Book of the Duchess* (1,334 lines), much longer than his next major effort, *The Parliament of Fowls* (694 lines). French poetry had always been his model, but it is clear that after his encounter with Italian poetry he was, as it were, trying to stretch his wings.

Perhaps that is why he found himself again attracted to birds. Here, as in the *Book of the Duchess*, he was writing with a specific occasion in mind, but this time the occasion was joyful. Between 1377 and 1382, there were repeated and finally successful attempts to arrange a marriage between young Richard II and Anne of Bohemia, daughter of Emperor Charles IV, and it is now widely accepted that Chaucer composed the poem to celebrate, or at least in connection with, that event. Towards the end of the poem, the formal (female eagle) is courted by a tercel (male eagle) who stands for Richard, and also by two lesser eagles, one of whom makes his claim on length of service, and so may be identified with Friedrich of Meissen, a German noble without a crown, who had been engaged to Anne for many years. If this is so, than it is likely that the even more noble eagle represents the French Dauphin, later King Charles VI of France, whose courtship, like Richard's, was of more recent date. It is usual to date the poem about June, 1380, since it was then that Friedrich's claims were still strong, but Chaucer was unlikely to have written, or to have been encouraged to write, before the issue was settled, and a date early in the 1380s seems at least as likely. *The Parliament of Fowls* has all the hallmarks of coterie production, of having been written for those for whom many among the congregation of birds, not just the eagles, would have been identifiable. The really remarkable thing is that this graceful, sophisticated, and witty poem reads as well as it does. It even opens with what has always seemed to me like a reference to the (now abandoned) *House of Fame*: "The life so sharp, the craft so long to learn," which certainly has other resonances too, and seems to refer as much to poetry as to love. Chaucer may still have been learning his craft, but he was about to make a leap. The next decade would see a simply extraordinary change in quantity and quality of his art. As far as Chaucer's poetry is concerned, the 1380s were like a Russian spring.

But not at first. The 1380s, the most complicated, problematic, and interesting decade in Chaucer's life, began with an event which even today scholars cannot really explain, let alone understand. On May 1, 1380, one Cecily Champain, the daughter of a baker, agreed to release Chaucer from all court actions *tam de raptu meo*, "concerning my rape," and three days later she appeared in person to affirm what had been written in her name.[7] Subsequently, she was paid £10 in consideration of her release, and while the money did not come from Chaucer directly, there is evidence (from his calling in outstanding obligations and the like) that it was the poet who paid. It is true that we do not know what it was all about, but the charge which had been brought against him was one of rape, and one technical meaning of the word seems to have been, then as now, forced and completed sexual relations. The events recorded seem more than anything to reflect, as Pearsall remarks, an affair which ended badly and perhaps with recrimination, and it is even possible that the £10 payment may have been associated with the birth of an unidentified child, whose existence would have proved that the affair was consummated, though that is pure conjecture. It also has all the hallmarks of class. Chaucer lined up five of his more substantial friends to support his side, the powerful court official Sir William Beauchamp, Admiral Sir William Neville, the devout author Sir John Clanvowe, John Philpot, like him a customs officer, and Member of Parliament Richard Morel. He paid Cecily Champain only months later, and then through an intermediary. The documents suggest an elaborate face-saving operation, and they also suggest at least a measure of guilt on Chaucer's part, a guilt he acknowledged, and paid quite a lot of money to suppress, or at least to be done with. It is important to remember how little we actually know about Chaucer's character or temperament, though the impression which, collectively, readers of his texts have garnered suggests a personally quiet but intellectually lively observer, who takes things as they come. But we really have no idea at all. There is even a second-hand and now lost account, first recorded in Thomas Speght's 1598 edition, which may have reported that the young poet beat up a Franscican friar in Fleet Street. However much we may come to like his poetry, we probably should not make Chaucer too saintly.

But whatever else they record, the Cecily Champain records certainly seem to indicate that by 1380 Chaucer had become a man of some substance. No longer was he simply the son of a successful wine merchant who had court connections: as he approached his fortieth year he had become a civil servant, and even a diplomat, of some importance. His position, achieved less through his connections than through his acuity and diligence, is important when set against a series of dramatic events which took place in the following year, the so-called "Peasants' Revolt" of 1381. The uprising of 1381 involved far more than the peasants to whom earlier generations of historians had assigned it, though it probably did begin with the 1377 poll tax, which had been reimposed in 1378 and again in 1381. But events began to take on a life of their own, and grievances which had been festering for years suddenly made themselves known: during two vital days, June 13–15, 1381, when those who had risen all but held much of London, important persons like John of Gaunt stood high on the list of those to be killed. The Savoy, John's palatial London residence, was sacked, and those who did so made a point of not looting, but rather chopping into pieces and throwing into the River Thames his plate and other valuables which they found there. Certain churchmen, particularly those allied with the court, became another target; Flemings, many of whom were murdered in London by a mob led by one "Jack Straw," another; lawyers and some civil servants as much as any of these.

But there also were two less personal targets: literacy and leadership. Literacy fixed debt and status forever (or so it seemed), and the destruction of records was an important part of the radical agenda. There was, too, the sense that young King Richard was being manipulated by those at court, as Anthony Goodman points out in his 1992 biography, like John of Gaunt, who was off negotiating at Berwick at the time of the uprising. But there was among those who had risen a respect for the nature of kingship itself, which was coupled to a sense that Richard's youth mitigated his personal culpability, and these led them to hold their hand and not slay Richard when they had their chance to do so. The 1381 revolt was finally put down through a mixture of overconfidence and naiveté on the part of those who had risen, and boldly duplicitous actions on the part of those threatened. In the midst of it all, young King Richard gallantly asserted his kingship and called upon the people to follow him away from a particularly dangerous confrontation, thus disarming a potentially disastrous situation. Soon afterwards, the king withdrew the concessions he had promised, but he also withdrew the poll tax, which had ignited events, and with it may have gone, for some among the rich, the sense of invulnerability which they had previously enjoyed.

Explicit references to the uprising in the *Canterbury Tales* are few and fleeting, though there is a reference to the murder of the Flemings in the *Nun's Priest's Tale*, and it is quite possible that the larger changes of which the revolt was both a cause and a symptom can be found throughout. Historically, however, students of Chaucer have not been accustomed to read or to interrogate his texts with such questions in mind, and the critical focus upon the persons and interchange of individual pilgrims in the *Canterbury Tales* has, until the development of powerful concerns like feminism, all but excluded less personal topics such as this one. In addition, Chaucer's fascination with class has further complicated his perhaps occasional interest in nationhood, against which his response to the social realities which underlay the 1381 revolt also stands.

Yet while it is true that, unlike his contemporary John Gower, Chaucer wrote no pointed and critical commentary on current conditions like the *Vox Clamantis* (circumspectly written in Latin), in dealing with pilgrims like the Reeve he did broach topics which many in his audience would perhaps be inclined to pass over. That is, he did not fail to represent the social and economic realities which the poor confronted, and to show their harshness. He was perhaps inclined to set against them the noble person of the Plowman or the writings of a pope, rather than any more modern and ideological construct, and how far these concerns extend in Chaucer is hard to say, though I shall return to them again in due course. But this is an important and relatively new dimension in the study of the *Canterbury Tales*, and is attached, in some degree, to the extensive studies now going forward on the 1381 uprising, and involving such complicating issues as literacy, nationhood, and class. It is as important an issue as there is now developing in Chaucer studies, and we should be aware of it, and reflect upon it, as we read his text.

It is not difficult to see however, even in the present state of scholarship, that the two events with which the decade of the 1380s began, the charge threatened in 1380 by Cecily Champain and the uprising of 1381, played directly upon Chaucer's art. His next poem represents a sea change from everything he had written before. *Troilus and Criseyde*, was based, sometimes closely, sometimes hardly at all, on Boccaccio's *Il Filostrato*, and was probably written between 1381 and 1386, 50 years after Boccaccio's work. It breaks with Chaucer's earlier writing in almost every way. Characters are complex, psychologically interesting, and grounded in reality. The events described are connected, rational, and important, and go to the very heart of the state – and the state of the heart. There is throughout a keen sense of the requirements which society necessarily imposes, and of the accommodations which individuals must therefore allow, but there is with it a sense of futility, a questioning not only of motivation but also of final purpose. The narrator now "weeps as I write," to tell the story of the young Trojan prince Troilus who is perhaps 16 years old, therefore old enough to be knighted and to take part in battles by fourteenth-century standards, when young men could be knighted even younger, particularly on the eve of battle. Troilus falls in love with, indeed surrenders himself to, Criseyde, who accepts him and his love, but who then is exchanged for a Trojan prisoner, Antenor, at the instigation of her father, Calkas, who already has deserted to the Greek camp, foreseeing that Troy's destiny is to fall. Troilus' devotion is absolute, but so is his youth, and in many ways he becomes little more than a plaything in the hands of crafty Pandarus, who in time brings about the much-desired consummation of his love, and indeed in the hands of Criseyde too, who in the beginning at least returns his love.

But it is his youth which not only makes him vulnerable to Criseyde's final betrayal, but concerned as well with Criseyde's honor, unable to speak up at the Trojan assembly where her exchange is debated, even when Hector opposes it. But Antenor is popular (this is ironic, since it is he who will later betray the city), and the exchange is agreed. Criseyde has arranged with Troilus to return to Troy in ten days' time, but during that time she is seduced by the Greek hero Diomede, who mixes treats and flattery, and more or less bullies Criseyde into becoming his lover. Criseyde writes of her change of heart to Troilus (she asks that they remain friends), and Troilus is finally convinced of her betrayal when a brooch which he has given her is taken from Diomede, though he cannot stop loving her even then. Troilus himself is subsequently killed by Achilles – Chaucer reports his death in one line – and his soul is taken up into the celestial spheres, there to laugh at his own past and at those who mourn it, before going where Mercury directs. But then Chaucer turns away from him, calling upon the young not to follow Troilus and his pagan belief in destiny, but to turn to God instead, who made him after his image, and placed him in a world which will soon pass away. He dedicates the book to "moral" John Gower, a landowning and excellent fellow-poet, and to "philosophical" Ralph Strode, a don at Merton College, Oxford, and a philosopher of real distinction, but he ends with a prayer which asks Christ who died on the cross (and so shared our suffering) to defend us, and so to make us worthy of salvation.

Chaucer's "little tragedy," as he calls *Troilus and Criseyde*, sounds themes and ideas which he had only touched on before, and it is difficult to escape the impression that not only his reading, but also his life, echo throughout. Chaucer needed no passing affair, whether painful, sad, or awkward, to realize in his poetry a sense of love betrayed, and no uprising to remind him that the state can be a fragile thing indeed, but both of these contingencies seem to have left their mark, difficult to define but easy to recognize, on the narrative tone and narrative voice which fills his pages. Gone is the final reliance upon literary authority, upon continental convention, even upon aristocratic audience, though all three are deeply implicated in his text. But what also distinguishes *Troilus and Criseyde* is that it is both "moral" and "philosophical" in a way Chaucer's early works were not. Chaucer's intellectual, as well as his courtly, friends have had their say in its composition, and there is a plain acknowledgment of that fact in the dedication. It may have been in the early 1380s (or possibly the late 1370s) that Chaucer translated the Latin philosopher Anicius Manlius Severinus Boethius (c.480–c.524) and began to develop the text which finally became the *Knight's Tale*, where Boethius' *Consolation of Philosophy* plays an important part. These influences, then, mixed with the sense of a suddenly vulnerable city, and the realization of the practical complications of love, to produce, in *Troilus*, a text unlike anything Chaucer had ever written before. What emerges is a steady and confident poetic voice, practiced and perceptive, a part of and yet apart from the literary practices of his time. Yet now again his life was about to change.

In 1386 Chaucer was serving as Justice of Peace when he was "elected" Knight of the Shire for Kent, though the word is some-

thing of a misnomer by modern standards, since his post was effectively the gift of the Sheriff. The result was that he came to sit in the
so-called "Wonderful Parliament" from the beginning of October
until the end of November, 1386, an extraordinary time in England.
It was during this period that young King Richard decided that he
was young no longer, and began to assume some of the powers
which appertain to kingship. Those who had been exercising them
in his name, however, were not amused. The issue was often cast in
terms of kingship and authority, and Richard had a way of using the
aura and dignity of his crown to secure loyalty and advantage. But it
didn't always work, particularly when, as now, the issue turned on
loose money and real power.

In order to escape the interference not only of an entrenched government bureaucracy but also of the Council which oversaw his
actions, Richard developed a circle of ennobled supporters – Chaucer
was *not* one of them – to help him stand against the party of opposition. But Richard's party included more than lords. The king was
not above, for example, forming an alliance with a food merchant
like Sir Nicholas Brembre, knighted for his services in 1381, an adversary of the then Lord Mayor of London, John of Northampton,
who had compelled Richard to allow into London certain previously
excluded merchants, thus driving down the price of food, and making friends and money for himself as well. In 1384 Brembre became
Lord Mayor, with the all-but-official backing of King Richard, who
thereupon withdrew some of the edicts to which Northampton had
caused him to assent. That he did so did not please those who had
been making money under the previous arrangements, but they had
other things to occupy them. During this time Richard sought to
make peace with France, thus ending another source of plunder
and adventure, and suggesting to them that this king was less manly
than his father, who had delighted in war. Two expeditions to Ireland, in 1395 and 1399, came too late to affect his reputation greatly.
There was also a mutual sense of grievance for slights received and
nobility overlooked, a sense that those opposing the king wanted
simply to maintain their prerogatives and power, and did not treat
him with the esteem they should, and that the king, for his part,
was high-handed and dismissive with any except those who were of
his party.

Finally, in November, 1387, the party in opposition had had

enough. Sensing themselves strong enough to do so, they brought appeals of treason against many in the king's own party, accusing them of treason against the king whom they served. Richard tried to delay things, but the two sides armed themselves, and a fierce encounter took place at Radcot Bridge on December 20, 1387, in which Henry Bolingbroke, who later deposed Richard II to become King Henry IV, utterly defeated a force led by the hated Robert de Vere, Earl of Oxford and Duke of Ireland. Thereafter Bolingbroke's party did as it pleased, using the law, which, during the so-called "Merciless Parliament" of 1388, it interpreted as it wished, to execute those in the king's party who had earned its enmity. These included, among others, Sir Nicholas Brembre and Thomas Usk, whose executions were nothing short of judicial murder. Subsequently, Commons passed a statute declaring, among other things, that all accusations, judgments, and executions of the Parliament of the time could not be used as precedents under common law in the future, and that no judge had authority to give judgments in cases of treason further than was done *before* the sitting of this Parliament. Parliament wanted to be sure that its own actions, particularly those relating to treason and forfeiture, could not be invoked against its own members at a later date. These extraordinary actions, the fine English historian M. V. Clark remarked acidly,[8] "proves that the irregularity of the whole proceedings was understood" (142).

We know from what Usk wrote about Chaucer that the two men knew each other, though how well is hard to say. Usk was the author of a prose treatise called *The Testament of Love*, which he probably wrote in prison, and which helps to date Chaucer's *Troilus*, to which it refers. But power, not art, was now the order of the day, and it must have given Geoffrey Chaucer a shock to see his colleague Thomas Usk's head displayed on a spike on London Bridge. These powerful ones who were opposing the king were playing for keeps.

After enough blood had been spilled some sense of normalcy returned, but only for a time. The party of opposition fell out among themselves, and John of Gaunt, ever a protector of King Richard, was recalled from his European adventures to lend a kind of stability to the crown. Richard was less aggressive in his behavior – understandably so, since so many of his closest supporters were banished, in hiding, or had been killed – but by 1390 he was active again, this time establishing the Order of the White Hart for those who would yet stand by him. But from 1389 until 1393 things were relatively quiet.

But whatever did Chaucer make of what was going on, and what part did he take in these events, in which, after all, he was clearly involved? In *Social Chaucer*,[9] a book which really for the first time set Chaucer and his work against the political realities of the period in which he lived, Paul Strohm detailed Chaucer's social and political attitudes during the late 1380s. Whereas in the past most scholars had thought that Chaucer stayed well away from politics, or at best kept a foot in both camps, Strohm argued that he had done no such thing, and that in certain important ways he was, at least for a period of time, Richard's man, though he also distanced himself to Richard, particularly as he became more despotic. Chaucer was, from the time he took up court appointments, regarded as an esquire of the king's household, *gentil* because of his appointment, but only just, one of a number of smart and able young men with connections but without noble blood, whom Richard recruited to his side with titles, blandishments and money. Strohm points out that Chaucer's status was not without ambiguity, and was shaped both by aristocratic and mercantile elements, but had its own special distinction, and enjoyed the informal status of gentility, albeit a gentility which allowed for annuities, fees, and offices. While other esquires, who, like Chaucer, were essentially landless, turned to military service to secure their new status, Chaucer, after becoming a member of the royal household in 1367, chose government service instead, though his military service under John of Gaunt in 1369 may have played a part in his advancement. He thus held a position, attached to the court and so to the king, which was at once widely recognized but without many precedents to guide him. He would, then, have to depend upon his wits and his connections, but there would be real prizes about if he could reach them.

The question of Chaucer's status, and his connection to the king, are of particular importance in the late 1380s, when Richard's crown came under threat. About this time he gave up his Controllership of Customs, and relinquished the lease on his house in Aldgate. He may have moved to Kent shortly before he did so. But why? Was it because he was too close to the king for comfort? After all, apart from his long association with John of Gaunt, one of Richard's chief props, he had been associated with many in the king's affinity during his years of service, including Sir Nicholas Brembre and (possibly at least) Thomas Usk. Was there a chance he might have to follow them to a place of execution? It is difficult to be sure, but probably not. Unlike them, Chaucer seems never to have played the power game, and much of the work entrusted to him had been painstaking and real, not make-work projects for someone with connections who needed a job. At the same time, it's hard to be sure. He got out of town (that is, probably moved to Kent) and, by giving up his lease, left in such a way that people would know he had really left for good, at least for now.

He may have resigned the appointments he did for political reasons (because he was seen as one of the king's men, who should now step back or be pushed aside), but in the 1390s his fortunes rose again – a little too quickly to believe that he had been in deep disgrace with either party beforehand. For one thing, at the end of the decade, his grants and offices were quickly approved under Henry IV, though Strohm is probably right to say that he had more trouble having them paid than having them approved. For another, early in the decade (about 1390) his friend and fellow poet John Gower dedicated the first recension of his great poem *Confessio Amantis* to Chaucer (VIII, 2941–57), and the same recension which praises Chaucer concludes with a prayer for King Richard, and 144 lines of more or less unstinting praise for his majesty, though in time Gower, like Chaucer, would come to moderate his enthusiasm. In the dedication to Chaucer, Venus refers to him as "my disciple and my poet," and remarks that in his youth the poet had made poems and verses for her sake with which the land was now full; now in advanced age she urges him, as "my own clerk," to write a "testament of love." There are thus indications that in the 1390s his reputation was becoming both broad and deep, at least among those who cared for English poetry.

It was during this period that the English crown left Richard II's head for that of Henry IV, however, and the change had implications even for an aging and esteemed court poet. In fact, the difficulty he had in actually getting paid after Henry had taken the throne may offer a further indication of his status. It is not unheard of for new administrations to be quicker in promising money than actually disbursing funds, and it is certainly possible that, in spite of

Chaucer's relative celebrity, his paperwork simply fell through the cracks. We really do not know. When enough (or too much) time had passed, however, the great poet finally wrote a short poem *The Complaint of Chaucer to His Purse* (the title humorously suggests a lover's complaint to his beloved), in which, among other things, he saluted the usurping King Henry IV as a "true king" (*verray kyng*), a sensitive point at the time. It got him his overdue payment almost at once. Throughout the incident, Chaucer certainly seems to have acted without the sort of personal arrogance associated with Sir Nicholas Brembre, and he had never sought to climb the slippery pole of simply political appointment which had attracted Thomas Usk. There is a temptation to see importance in any piece of hard evidence we have concerning Chaucer's career, and, in the extraordinary tempests of 1388 he may indeed have had to trim his sails. Like everyone who survived in public life, Chaucer had to keep his wits about him, but probably the most trying time during this period came in 1387, when Philippa, his wife of 22 years, died.

As so often when we look to medieval authors for evidence of felt, human relationships, we are reduced to hints and implications. But it is now generally agreed that it was at about this time, after he had written *Troilus and Criseyde*, that he wrote (but never completed) *the Legend of Good Women*, at least in part to make up for the unsympathetic representation of Criseyde's inconstancy which the god of love (in the *Legend*) chides him with. "Leave the chaff and write well about the corn," the god urges him, and this is what the poet-narrator sets out to do. In former times, scholars used to think that the work was not "good enough" to come this late in the poet's career, and that he had written it as early as the 1370s; now we know that it is very good indeed, although, as is the case with so many of Chaucer's texts, we are not sure exactly when it was written.

Still, it may possibly be associated with the death of his wife, though Chaucer was no Carlyle, and whether Philippa's death caused him to write the work, or to break off, we do not know; quite possibly neither, it must be said. But, along with a quick intellectual playfulness, and a readiness both to present anti-feminist ideas and then to mock them, there is also a tone of elegy, a sense of loss and even intimacy, which may owe less to the audience before him than the one he has lost. He says he will tell many a "story" and many a "geste" (a true history), in this work, but in the end he tells only nine, and leaves the work incomplete. But it is no little thing. The text as we have it is 2,723 lines long, and apart from *Troilus*, it was his longest work to date. "Trust no man but me," he ironically insists, knowing that we do, and won't. But he does not abandon his interest, his concern, for women, and will return to these themes repeatedly throughout the *Canterbury Tales*, as we shall see.

We do not know exactly when Chaucer began to organize the *Canterbury Tales*, but it was probably sometime after 1387, after, that is, the death of his wife, and possibly after 1389, when Richard II had effectively regained his throne, the divisions among the lords opposing him having given him some breathing room, if only for a time. More or less obviously, he drew on a number of tales he had already written, and added others. This is a complex and vexing problem for any editor of the *Tales*, and lies outside the orbit of this book. If you become interested in the issue, an article by Larry Benson is probably a good place to begin.[10] But it was during this period that it became clear that Chaucer had indeed survived treacherous times. In 1389 he was appointed Clerk of the King's Works, which included responsibilities for overseeing construction and repair work on royal properties at Westminster and also at the Tower of London, no easy job. In the following year, 1390, he was appointed Commissioner of Walls and Ditches, a most responsible position (though it may not sound so to a modern ear), one that gave him oversight responsibility for public works along the River Thames between Woolwich and Greenwich.

These were not make-work appointments. They required real effort and organizational ability, such as Chaucer had shown during his years at the customs house, so much so that one reason for not identifying Chaucer too closely with the King's Affinity, with those nobles and others who supported and attended upon King Richard, was the offices which he held. Appointments they may have been, and Paul Strohm's suggestion in *Social Chaucer* that Chaucer was a member of the *mesnals gentils*, originally a member of the household, subsequently an esquire in service to the king (21) is useful, but the offices which Chaucer came to hold required enough diligence to make the office-holder finally more dependent upon his own effectiveness than upon the king's grace. It was not that members of the King's Affinity, and others who supported Richard, did not perform difficult, even onerous, duties. But they rarely filled offices which played less upon the person of the king than upon the administrative work at hand, and that effectively put some space between Chaucer and the king he served. As Clerk of the King's Works, Chaucer had among his duties to oversee payments to what we would call today contractors, and also to pay the workmen, duties which involved some risk. On September 3, 1390, Chaucer was robbed of over £20 of the king's money, his own horse and other valuables as well at Hatcham, in Kent (he seems then to have been living in Kent). Three days later, if the record can be believed, he was robbed again, this time of £10, and not in the countryside, but in Westminster itself.

These events may have had an influence upon a decision the following November to call Chaucer in for an audit, which revealed that he had overspent by more than £20. This was no big deal: Chaucer had used his own funds, according to common practice, to balance the books and allow for the spending, but, taken together with the robberies, it may have suggested to those in charge that it was time for a change, and that Chaucer, loyal and trusted as he was, should be put to less demanding work. In any event, on June 17, 1392, he was instructed to give up his post as Clerk of the King's Works, and the 2 shillings a day wage that went with it, to one John Gedney. He did so, quite possibly with relief.

Still, he needed paid employment, and none was immediately forthcoming. Over the next few months he was able to collect debts which the government owed him as a result of his work, and then at some time, probably in the early 1390s, he was appointed Deputy Forester of the Royal Forest in North Pemberton, Somerset (a post which, after his death, his son Thomas was to hold, though not direct from his father). The records of his work there are few and late, and we do not know what he did, though there is no reason to think that he had to travel often to Somerset, still less to live there. He may well have been able to undertake such duties as there were from London, but we really do not know. After that, things got better still. On February 28, 1394, he was granted an annual annuity of £20, in effect a pension, and then on December 1, 1397 King Richard granted the poet a tun of wine (252 gallons) annually, not as much as the daily pitcher King Edward had awarded him in 1374, perhaps, but a right kingly gift, in any case.

Throughout this period, then, the period in which he would become deeply engaged in writing the *Canterbury Tales*, the picture which emerges is one of a poet who has put much of his government work behind him, who is on reasonably firm ground financially, and who is well known and respected in the court. We know that he drew upon earlier compositions in organizing his great work, and that certain of the tales – the *Knight's Tale*, for example, and probably also the *Prioress's Tale*, and the *Second Nun's Tale* – were rewritten from earlier versions, and that others – the *Canon's Yeoman's Tale*, and possibly the *Monk's Tale* and the *Parson's Tale* – show evidence of earlier composition too, if not so compellingly. It is at least possible then, that after 1391 Chaucer found himself with more time that was his own. He may then have got on with a project which, however much it owed to French poets, really began decades earlier, in his father's house in London, when, in conversation with Italian merchants, he had first heard the name Boccaccio.

Probably many readers of this book will at least have heard of Richard II from Shakespeare's play of the same name. That play presents a not very attractive picture of a failed monarch, a little too concerned with the way he is seen and addressed, given to underestimating his well-meaning adversaries, feeling that he is really above it all, when in fact he is simply making a mess of things. The real Richard was a very different kettle of fish, though there are elements in Shakespeare's description which ring true. Still, this was the king who, at the age of fourteen, confronted those who had risen up against him in 1381 with courage and aplomb, and survived the blows received from the Lords who opposed him seven years later. But Richard was never happy with the arrangements which were arrived at in 1388, and in 1397 decided it was time to strike back. In August of that year he had four of his principal opponents arrested. One of these was subsequently murdered under circumstances which suggest Richard's involvement, one sent for execution, and two condemned to exile. Another opponent was subsequently killed in Ireland, and two others, Thomas Mowbray, the duke of Norfolk and Henry Bolingbroke, the duke of Hereford, sent into exile, but not until they had fallen out between themselves so dramatically that on September 16, 1398, they were forced to resort to a trial by combat to prove their loyalty to Richard. In the end Richard stopped the combat, and sent them both into exile instead. It proved to be his fatal mistake, but it was perhaps not one he could have easily avoided.

Still, it did not seem so at the time. To all appearances, by the end of September, 1398, Richard emerged from his campaign altogether victorious over his enemies, and utterly secure on his throne. It may have been about this time that Chaucer wrote a poem which is at once enigmatic and commonplace, now usually called "Lak of Stedfastness." An early scribe, John Shirley, had noted that Chaucer wrote the poem "in his last years," and the tone of it suggests that he did so at a time when Richard held the upper hand (and could so be urged to action), so that 1398 would be a very possible date. If it was then that Chaucer wrote it, the poem may be somewhat less conventional than is usually believed, since Richard was not a king who encouraged criticism (few did). The acknowledgment of the kingdom's failings is presented as something that a bold king can still put right, which was true only for a relatively short time. But then on February 3, 1399, John of Gaunt died, and everything changed forever. John had been Richard's supporter, even when it became apparent to everyone that Henry Bolingbroke, his son by his first wife, was working against Richard. John's past support, which was indeed valuable, made it impossible simply to have Harry executed, and with John of Gaunt still alive, Richard imposed an exile on Henry of only six years, and promised that, once his father John of Gaunt had died, Henry could keep his inheritance, rich estates in Lancaster. At the time, it was the course which seemed clearly indicated. He did not wish to lose John of Gaunt's support by being too hard on his wayward son, and if he had Henry executed, he would indeed have seemed to be a tyrant. But he took the measure of the man, and knew that he was dangerous. That was why, after John's death, he changed Henry's sentence to perpetual banishment and then on March 18, 1399, seized the estates in Lancaster for the crown. Then at the end of May, in an extraordinary misjudgment, he left England to campaign in Ireland.

At the end of the next month Harry returned in force to England, in order to secure his inheritance, he said, though there is no doubt he had greater plans in mind as well. He received much support from friends old and new, and when Richard rushed back in July, he found himself with no choice but to accept the assurances Henry sent him, and to accept things as they were. But on September 30 he was forced to abdicate, and on October 13 Henry Bolingbroke was crowned King Henry IV. Richard's fate thereafter was summarized by Jane Austen in her childhood *History of England* (1791) in this opening sentence: "Henry the 4th ascended the throne of England much to his own satisfaction in the year 1399, after having prevailed on his cousin and predecessor Richard the 2nd, to resign it to him, and to retire for the rest of his life to Pomfret Castle, where he happened to be murdered."

Chaucer survived the transition of government with surprising ease. A document confirming and even increasing Chaucer's annual pension was forthcoming, though backdated to the day of Henry's coronation. But however deep his personal or professional attachment to Richard may have been, Chaucer was never in any danger under the new regime. Quite apart from his age, quite apart from his established reputation for public duty and for English poetry, quite apart even from his connection, through his wife, to the Lancastrian cause, there was also the unassailable fact that for many years Chaucer himself had been associated, as a supporter and more importantly as a client, with John of Gaunt, the new king's father. His connections to Richard could easily be viewed as administrative and professional, not personal. When all was said and done, he was as firmly in Henry's camp as he ever had been in Richard's.

We know very little about Chaucer's last days. On December 24, 1399, he took a lease on a tenement in the garden of the Lady Chapel of Westminster Abbey, which was almost certainly the place he was living when he died. The fact that he held the tenancy meant that he would be buried in the Abbey, and it is possible that that fact influenced his choice. On February 21, 1400, and again on June 5, royal payments were made to Geoffrey Chaucer, but, contrary to his custom, he did not appear to collect them in person, and it is possible that he was unwell during this time. The date of his death is usually given as October 25, 1400, and though it is to some extent arbitrary, it does not seem to be wildly mistaken.

As was appropriate to one of his position, standing, and residence, he was buried in Westminster Abbey, at first very modestly, by the entrance to St. Benedict's chapel, but then in 1556 his remains were moved to a new tomb in the south transept. In death as in art other poets followed him, so that the place in the Abbey where he lies is now known as "Poets' Corner." Throughout his career he had taken a largely unstoried language and given it a power and authority it had not enjoyed before, placing it on an equal footing with any European literature. At the time of his death he was certainly the greatest poet England had yet produced, and there is every reason to believe that many of his contemporaries understood his celebrity. Yet he left his greatest work, the *Canterbury Tales*, unfinished. And it is to it that we shall now turn.

2

Gender and Religion, Race and Class

A text like the *Canterbury Tales* raises many questions which Chaucer never anticipated, and in order to answer them readers often "interrogate" Chaucer's tales, seeking to identify attitudes and ideas which are not immediately apparent, but which are implicit, not explicit, in the narratives. This means that "the author's intention" in writing the text cannot be taken as the only thing to interest a reader. After all, reading is itself a substantial action, and one which involves not only the engagement of values, but also a rejection, or at least a questioning, of some of them. Reading thus is no more passive than those other acts of interrogation to which it gives birth, and it is certainly possible to read both text and author, recalling that it is the reader who finally negotiates between them. Texts like the *Canterbury Tales* invariably reveal a sense of difference in matters which engage us still, though the author who inscribed it would remain something of a mystery even if he had lived just six years ago, not six hundred.

But it is equally possible to fetishize cultural difference, so that finally nothing is thought to be known or knowable, and the only authority is whatever construction – of philosophy, history, psychology, or biology – I choose to employ. Reading has always involved negotiation, and that is at least part of what many students of literature continue to call the pleasure of reading a text. Additionally, if the author (or the concept of an author) is excluded from critical discourse, then the concept of the author's gender must go with it, and with that the basis for developing the role and significance of gender in a text. But this is exactly what we must not exclude, par-

The Squire (Hodnett No. 219)

ticularly in an author like Chaucer where such concerns are privileged. The issues which engage us now are indeed different than those of an earlier century – the twentieth no less than the fourteenth – but it is we who must address them.

In Chaucer's own day, and for some time thereafter, his defense of women, indeed his championing of them, was never in doubt. The traditional image of the poet as "Venus' own clerk" was reinforced by the testimony of those who shortly followed him, like the fifteenth-century Scottish translator of Virgil, Gavin Douglas, who recorded in the Prologue to that work that Chaucer "was ever, God knows, all women's friend," though in the same breath he objected to Chaucer's unsympathetic representation of Aeneas as a false and deceitful lover in the *Legend of Good Women*. But what form did that putative friendship take? In a consideration of the role of patristic and other texts which informed his fictions, Carolyn Dinshaw takes a very different approach, noticing how he used patristic, not classical, sources, and remarking, in *Chaucer's Sexual Poetics*,[1] that "Chaucer attempts to discern the consequences for literature and literary tradition, and the effects on lived lives, of understanding literary endeavor as masculine acts performed on feminine bodies." But even when his sources were classical, Dinshaw notes, a masculine narrator "engages with his pagan source texts as if they were women, treats them in ways analogous to the ways in which male lovers in the narratives treat their women" (25). Dinshaw is not the first critic to read the action of writing in explicitly sexual terms, and her description of a Christian commentator glossing the Bible as an action which is "unmistakably carnal, a masculine act performed on the feminine body" (125), serves as a starting point for an analysis which involves a discussion of the *Legend of Good Women* in terms very different from those of Gavin Douglas. In this reading, unattractive and deceitful male characters like Aeneas

> are unvarying, nothing but opportunistic scoundrels in love, and the "moralitee" of each fable is a truism. The techniques of reading like a man – imposing a single pattern, insisting on reducing complexity to produce a whole, monolithic structure, thus constraining the feminine – are reductive of *all* human experience ... reading like a man leads to no literary activity at all. (87)

Readings like this one (one of the earlier feminist interpretations of the *Canterbury Tales*) made clear how important a consideration gender is throughout Chaucer, and some of the following chapters will develop these concerns, though Dinshaw's awareness of the sense of multiplicity in Chaucer, of the ways in which the complexity of many of these concerns become apparent more in their interrelationships than separately, is important to keep in mind, even by those who are uneasy with the idea that the way of reading thus described is invariably – or essentially – masculine. In considering what Chaucer's attitudes may have been toward any of these concerns, it is important to remain aware of the pervasive possibilities of authorial detachment, irony and humor.

Chaucer's attention to gender is thus both apparent and widespread, but it is rarely totalizing, and is usually attached to other preoccupations, including those of religion and class. A later chapter will address this subject at some length, noticing, for example, how certain of the pilgrims – the Prioress, the Nun's Priest, the Second Nun – develop a discourse concerning the ways in which persons perceive and cooperate with the divine in advancing human affairs, and in the case of the Second Nun, it is a discourse in which gender figures importantly. Thus, although gender and religion often intersect and Chaucer often implies that many of the values which women honor are at heart religious, he does not assume that religious values can be identified only with women. What he urges instead is that religious values are most apparent, and most attractive, not only among those like the Parson whose office and character combine to testify to his religiousness, but also among the marginalized, those who have not the power to enforce their will, and that women are sometimes among those so described. Even when dealing with commanding women, like St. Cecilia, a Roman noble in the *Second Nun's Tale*, Chaucer insists that her authority, bonded to her gender as it is, finally resides in her faith rather than in her class, and that it is that which animates her.

In an example which avoids any suggestion of Christian religiousness, Chaucer describes a woman of particular power and energy in the person of Zenobia, the historical third-century queen of Palmyra who, after holding much of the Eastern Empire in the name of Rome after her husband's suspicious death, rebelled and tried to establish her own throne, but was finally defeated by the Roman Emperor Aurelian in AD 272, who returned her to Rome in chains, there to appear in his triumph. The Monk describes Zenobia's career and downfall in an account heavily dependent upon Boccaccio's *De mulieribus claris,* written between 1361 and 1362.[2] Like Boccaccio's Zenobia, Chaucer's "Cenobia" is powerful and successful at least in part because of her physical strength and personal discipline. Chaucer notes that her origins were Persian where Boccaccio had written Ptolmaic, and though the alteration may be the result of a simple slip (elsewhere Chaucer refers to Petrarch where he meant to write Boccaccio), references to Persians in Boccaccio as famous for their prowess in battle and their wit and cordiality may have led Chaucer to make the change deliberately, both in the interests of his untraveled audience, and so as to link his powerful and impressive queen even more tightly to the East. There are other differences as well. Though Boccaccio's Zenobia, like Chaucer's, allows her husband to lie with her "but once" until she learned whether or not she was with child, Chaucer's receives no narrative commendation for this action, in spite of the fact that such praise might be expected of the Monk narrator. Equally, her account in Chaucer describes her conquests and exploits in far less detail than the one in Boccaccio, de-emphasizing the state in which, in spite of her personal abstemiousness she lived (though mentioning the richness of her dress), and emphasizing instead the suddenness of her fall in terms which suggest vulnerability as well as ill fortune. Though the text emphasizes her virtues, identified as male, and never suggests that she is being punished for acting outside of what the nineteenth century called a "woman's sphere," Chaucer holds back from a wholehearted endorsement of her values and attitudes, even as he acknowledges her prowess, strength, and nobility.

But Chaucer could be critical of these values, too, and throughout the *Canterbury Tales* he seems to have treated the subject of being a man with at least as much ambiguity as he did that of being a woman. In one particularly piquant phrase, he describes the Monk in the *General Prologue* as "A manly man, to be an abbot able / Ful many a fine horse had he in his stable ..." (167–8), though his description of the Plowman, "A true worker and a good was he / Living in peace and perfect charity" (531–2), forms a kind of balance to this description, particularly when Chaucer stresses the Plowman's willingness to undertake hard, physical labor: "For Christ's sake, for every poor person, / Without pay, if it lay within his power" (537–8). But it is with some of his more ambiguous characters that Chaucer's attitude towards maleness becomes most apparent, and nowhere more so than in his almost riddling description of the Shipman (388–410).

One of the very few characters in the *Canterbury Tales* who seems almost certainly formed by a mixture of historical memory, personal experience, and a modified version of events recorded in Chaucer's own biography, is the Shipman, still one of the less studied and least attractive of the pilgrims, whose complex and indubitably male background requires a word of explanation. He was first studied in John M. Manly's *Some New Light on Chaucer*,[3] where Manly notes a connection to one John Hawley, the second of that name, a rough contemporary of Chaucer's who died in 1408, and whom Chaucer almost certainly met in 1373, though Manly felt that Hawley was "too wealthy, distinguished, and perhaps too courtly a person" (178) actually to have supplied the model. Even so, this is one of the very few times when Chaucer seems to have allowed his own experience to figure in his fiction. In August of that year, recently back from a trip to Italy and conversant in Italian, Chaucer was sent by King Richard II to arrange for the release of a Genoese ship which John Hawley had captured, and was holding. Hawley, a larger than life character, was four times Member of Parliament and fourteen times mayor of Dartmouth in Devon, occupations which he combined with a certain amount of piracy, too, events now familiar from having been recorded in the English Heritage guidebook to Dartmouth Castle and in Terry Edwards's *Hawley's Fortalice*.[4] Manly was right to say that Hawley was not "the original" of Chaucer's Shipman, whose character probably emerged out of Chaucer's reflection upon Hawley and the men he commanded, and perhaps too upon that of the previous mayor, William Smale, who is actually recorded as having drowned prisoners he took at sea. In time, John Hawley became trusted enough by the crown so that, in spite of events in 1373, he was in 1379 licensed as a privateer and in 1388, as mayor, entrusted to construct a small protective fort at the mouth of the River Dart, the first of Dartmouth's several castles. Hawley gained great fame three years after Chaucer's death, when, in 1403, he repelled a Breton reprisal raid for one of Hawley's own raids into Brittany. King Henry IV ordered a *Te Deum* mass sung in celebration of the event in London, but that did not prevent him, three years later, from imprisoning Hawley in the Tower of London until he promised to restore some plunder he had seized. Hawley is buried in a thirteenth-century Dartmouth church now known as St. Saviour's, under a magnificent brass which shows him in full armor and between his two wives. Appropriately, his grave is situated in the center of the eastward extension of the church, a rebuilding which he himself had paid for, no doubt from his plunder.

   In his day Hawley was notorious, and he certainly figures in the composition of the militantly male character whom Chaucer calls the Shipman, though they are not the same man. Chaucer specifically mentions the Shipman's association with Dartmouth, a place notorious for following its own ways and for piracy, though the man's unkempt dress, the dagger hanging around his neck, his tanned face and difficulty on horseback all seem calculated to lower his stature (and his class), and to make him seem less impressive than Hawley himself struck his contemporaries. But his skill and success in battle, undertaking and storm ("Tough he was, and prudent in what he did"), his practiced seamanship, his easy conscience, the apparent nonchalance with which he drowns his captives ("By water he sent them home to every land"), all point to a more able and powerful character than the opening lines suggest. The references to Finisterre and to Brittany point towards Hawley, whose adventures thereabouts were famous, though some scholars believe that the actual identity of *Fynystere* remains in doubt. Manly was much impressed with the fact that there were contemporary ships named (as his is) the *Maudelayne*, which operated out of, or at least were associated with, Dartmouth, but that the Shipman's vessel should be named for a repentant prostitute will surprise no one who has followed the course of John Hawley's career, and noted the twisted and ambiguous definition of maleness which he holds out. The Shipman is thus another of Chaucer's "manly men," like the Monk, whose life at once defines and indicts his gender, and if Chaucer turns away from too obvious an identification with Hawley, he embraces and records the mayor-pirate's ambiguous reputation, his (or at least his predecessor's) murderous practices, even his apparently disarming mixture of villain and hero. What matters too is the way in which Chaucer has used his character to bring home, at least in the *General Prologue*, the murderous ways of the sea, and the men who sail it. In doing so he did not write as a literary realist, and it is certainly a mistake to seek "an original" for any of his Pilgrims. But the Shipman reminds us again that his narratives are not so much a "reflection" of society as they are an interpretive and analytic act of processing it, formulating and even creating the social and fictional reality from which, paradoxically, they spring, so that gender and violence, history and class, figure repeatedly in their construction.

Yet it is not surprising that, interesting though the Shipman's putative history may be, the man himself seems hardly worthy of his tale, which is at once polished and coarse, sophisticated and crude. This disjunction between Pilgrim and narrative is further complicated by the fact that the narrative voice can at times be identified as that of a woman, and the usual explanation of this fact is that it was originally assigned to the Wife of Bath. But the tale is also a type, one named by Helen Cooper in *The Structure of the Canterbury Tales*[5] "the girl with two lovers" (227), and as such has affinities to the tales told by the Miller, the Merchant, and the Knight. The affinities are not only in the narrative structure Cooper described, the girl with two lovers, they are also in the pattern of images which run throughout, and which here as elsewhere in Chaucer qualify, describe further, or sometimes undermine that narrative structure. One of the more important of these images is that of the woman in the garden, reminiscent of Eve, and the mood of temptation, or at least of enticement, which she and the garden hold out. In the *Shipman's Tale* a licentious and manipulative monk walks in the garden with the wife of a merchant who pays too much attention to his accounts, and closes his eyes to what is going on around him. In the *Merchant's Tale* an old knight, blind in more sense than one, secures his very young wife in a garden to which he foolishly believes he has the only key: he thinks he will mold her like wax, but she herself has already used wax to fashion another key so that her lover can join them there. In the *Knight's Tale* Emily walks alone in her garden, blind to the affection of two young knights imprisoned in a tower, who are equally blind to the narrowness of their own gaze. Finally, in the *Miller's Tale*, the garden has shrunk either to an enclosed room where Nicholas, an Oxford student, and Alison, the Miller's wife, can speak and wrestle together, or worse, to three large tubs hung from the rafters by ropes.

Notice that these tales are otherwise unconnected: the Knight does not speak to the Miller, though the tale the Miller tells is clearly a parody of the Knight's, nor does the Merchant address the Shipman, though their occupations are connected: without shipping the Merchant can no more survive than could the Shipman, without commerce to carry or plunder. The structural link which draws these tales together, a girl and two lovers, pushes them apart, as well. Four women could hardly be more different, eight lovers more chaotic. But in spite of everything, a sense of gender defamed, manipulated, and enjoyed runs through the tales, almost as though Chaucer was trying and re-trying a simple formula to find the time it works. He experiments with persons but does so by setting them against a frozen landscape – one girl, two lovers – which will at once dictate and frustrate their every move. Not Fate, not Providence, but only the writer's fingers can make a change, though against an aesthetic where constructions last, the twists of chance and circumstance seem written large.

But against literary artifice stand the facts of history, another way to read these changing tales. *The Age of Saturn. Literature and History in the Canterbury Tales,*[6] a collaborative book by Peter Brown (a literary scholar) and Andrew Butcher (an archivist and historian) took chances other studies didn't. In one of its more controversial passages it suggested that the relationship in the *Merchant's Tale* between an old knight, January, and his young bride, May, would have been widely recognized in the English court as an ironic and comic representation of the relationship between the old king Edward III and his young mistress Alice Perrers, and furthermore, that that relationship came to stand, in the eyes of Chaucer's audience, for the political crisis which only the young King Richard II could address.

Like all good historians, Brown and Butcher are attentive to details. At one point Justinus, a friend of January whose office is suggested by his name, says this to January, who is intent on marrying a partner whom everyone but he knows to be unsuitable:

> As things turn out, she may be your purgatory!
> She may be God's means and God's whip:
> Then shall your soul up to heaven skip
> Swifter than does an arrow out of a bow.

"Employing the teachings of contemporary Canon Law," Brown and Butcher remark:

> Justinus' argument suggests an understanding of the crisis of the 1370's which sees Alice Perrers as a divine agent in a necessary process of punishment and purification. The decision of January to disregard the advice of friends, counsellors, church and commons, is to break the holy bonds of constitutional matrimony and to release a purgatory of self-destructive policies and conflicts. (200)

Of course, this interpretation requires the modern reader to believe that a quite extraordinary degree of freedom of expression, or aristocratic sophistication, existed in King Edward's court (or soon thereafter), and that Chaucer's position was secure enough to allude to what may have been rather sensitive matters more or less as it suited him. But whatever degree of credence we attach to empirical considerations, these readings share more than a kind of critical audacity. They both are equally willing to read Chaucer's evident fascination with women against psychological or historical considerations which gender and sex reveal: sexual attachments inform court gossip, and sometimes the reverse, so that, reading the *Canterbury Tales*, you should be alert to the ways in which, consciously or not, Chaucer allows gender and sex, position and status, social circumstance and providential intervention, mutually to inform his fictions. There are no rules here, but there are opportunities, and, brilliant writer that he is, Chaucer makes the most of them. So can you.

Probably the single most difficult topic to write about in Chaucer concerns his attitudes toward race – though like many of his readers, I sometimes wish that it was harder still. The difficulty is that there are times throughout the *Canterbury Tales* when it seems entirely clear that Chaucer's attitude toward what we now would unhesitatingly call race is at once very difficult and very easy to understand. I will discuss certain aspects of this attitude in the chapters which follow, though it is probably right that, in some cases which look like racism to the modern reader, Chaucer would say that he was concerned with traditional adversaries of Christianity, pagans, Jews, and Muslims, and was really defending his faith, not attacking another without reason. But this sort of defense is no longer very convincing – for one thing, the history of the twentieth century, and even the first years of the twenty-first, have already supplied examples of racial hostility which pretends to be religious – as if that would make it any better. But it is good to be attentive whenever Chaucer writes about non-Christians of whatever sort, since it is then that some of the less attractive social attitudes, widely present in his period, present themselves, and not always in a context which suggests irony or authorial distance. In 1986[7] Gerald Morgan remarked in a discussion of the "moral dilemma" (285) in the *Franklin's Tale*, that "action and not character is everywhere dominant in medieval and in Chaucerian art, and that the principal of action is the artistic idea" (288). This reading may seem in one way to free Chaucer from the sometimes invidious representations which his characters present – Morgan is careful to point out the importance of such apparently irrelevant digressions as the long complaints in the *Franklin's Tale*, which he perceptively takes to be the pillars which actually sustain the tale, since it is these which define the thought-world through which the characters move. But the actions which the characters perform do not always do them credit, and it is probably a good idea to remember the ways in which these medieval artistic conventions can inform narrative structures.

Because there are elements of a kind of apparently modern realism in many of Chaucer's tales, particularly his use of individual details in particular scenes, it is sometimes easy to forget the more powerful cultural and contextual concerns which equally inform them, so that in recent years it has become easy for some critics to denounce Chaucer for formulating concerns with such issues as race in terms which, at face value, are certainly very unattractive. But many of his narrative choices have a cultural component which is at least as important as the personal or psychological one – and in medieval texts, the cultural component can predominate. Thus Chaucer is often in dialogue with the cultural conventions of his period, and though sometimes, as when he deals with antisemitism, it is easy to wish that his position was more progressive – by which I mean more modern – than it in fact is, he seems usually to objectify the received positions which he represents, to hold them out at arm's length for inspection and even analysis. And yet the difference between the times he is doing so, and the times he is simply representing things as he understood them to be, is sometimes very difficult to ascertain.

In the chapters which follow I have sometimes indicated when Chaucer seems to me to be involved in a kind of critical dialogue which is attached more to issues than to persons, but it is probably worth saying that sometimes he is not, and that it is when he is dealing with matters of religion that he appears most constrained. It is not difficult to believe that this constraint, encouraged by the forms of ecclesiastical scrutiny and practice available to him, informed the working out of his attitudes towards what we would now call race. But the kinds of practical narrowness and intellectual (and physical) resistance to those who are defined as other, can reasonably be seen as rooted in some of the same religious constructions which equally apply to the social and doctrinal changes and corruptions which he everywhere describes. In matters of religion, Chaucer was not finally a relativist, and if his perceptions were quite unsparing in their identification of what was false, they were equally so in their understanding of who was ours, and who was other.

But if there was a level in Chaucer's mind as felt as religion, that level was probably class. This is one of the most powerful categories present throughout the *Canterbury Tales*, but like gender, like race, it did not exist in isolation. When we read in the *Knight's Tale* that "Pity runs soon in a gentle heart," it is important to realize that Chaucer means what he says: pity, that quality of which invokes sympathy, understanding, insight comes naturally to the noble heart, and hardly ever to one which is not noble. True enough, Chaucer also questions the whole concept of nobility – "Christ directs that we claim our nobility from him," a character in the *Wife of Bath's Tale* brilliantly insists, "not because we have noble ancestors, or old money." But for many readers that proud assertion, which must have given a moment's discomfort to some at least in Chaucer's first audience, makes him ours. But be wary when you read: Chaucer was not a twenty-first-century democrat, and it is important not to make him into one. The passage in the *Wife of Bath's Tale* does not contest the basic concept of nobility, after all, indeed it confirms it, though it does so from a somewhat unusual position. In the *Second Nun's Tale* the protagonist, St. Cecilia, is a Roman noblewoman, but it is her actions, not the accident of her birth, which Chaucer approves. Still, as he does so, it is just possible to believe that she is by her actions living up to her birth, which may not be an accident at all. In fact there was a tradition of writing saints lives for a group of women usually designated as virgin martyrs – St. Catherine, St. Dorothy, St. Margaret of Antioch, for example – all of whom (like Chaucer's St. Cecilia) were executed by a pagan judge (or emperor), and all of whom were members of the nobility. Gender, class, religion and race tended to overlap in the period, and they do so in Chaucer, too. It is thus useful to be aware of the power and effectiveness of the concept of class (like those of gender and race, it rarely exists in isolation) throughout the *Canterbury Tales*, and to be attentive to its quick, sometimes fleeting appearances, to the values and attitudes it both rests upon and perpetuates, and to its easy agreement with what the audience expects and assumes.

It is not so much the identity of any one of these categories which is difficult to understand, but the ways in which they interact, and perhaps above all the things they take for granted. Gender responded to class, but had too its own integrity, an integrity which Chaucer often represents as attached to religion. Righteous judgment in matters ecclesiastical, social and literary rested upon an ability to separate the true from the false, and that upon an understanding of who "we" were. These powerful and important values, concerns, beliefs, attitudes, and assumptions course throughout the *Canterbury Tales*, and it is important, as Emerson says, to name them as you find them.

3

Others

Because medieval culture is often represented as compact and even closed, a world where everyone both knew and kept to his or her place, and where social change, when it took place at all, was usually the result of war, natural catastrophe, revolution, or plague, the importance of outsiders to that culture, of aliens or of "others," has been a relatively recent scholarly interest, but one which has thrown a sharp and sometimes hard light on what Chaucer and his contemporaries thought about those who were unlike them.

The *Canterbury Tales* is more than a series of tales told by a fictional group of pilgrims on their way to worship at the shrine of St. Thomas of Canterbury. In a different way it *is* that reality. The putative "world" of the *Canterbury Tales* is not of Nature's making, but of Chaucer's, and his constructions contain both deformities and occasional flashes of brilliance which should neither be taken at face value, nor thought of as *simply* reflecting "how things really were." Like most of us, Chaucer mediated such social reality as he knew, and it is that mediated reality which his art preserved. That is what we see: not an "objective" social reality which the *Canterbury Tales* represents, or tries to. We see rather a refracted reference, so that the text itself is part of that world, as is its now almost depersonalized author, known to every student, whether they have read him or not, as "Chaucer." The distance between London and Canterbury, 54 miles, may be only an hour or so by car, but it is a long ride on horseback. The pilgrims have banded together for protection, but with an armed knight along (small wonder he has the authority he does to intervene against the Pardoner, the Monk, and even Harry

The Friar (Hodnett No. 219)

Bailey himself), they have reason to feel secure. Chaucer certainly allows that they have come for many reasons, some because of a vow made to St. Thomas that they would visit his shrine if he would help them recover from a winter sickness, others as an excursion, others like the pilgrim Chaucer himself, with sincere Christian devotion.

I have said that we really do not know very much about when Chaucer began to write any individual tale, or even when he began work on the collection as a whole. It is clear that he left the collection unfinished (in his "chest") when he died, so we can say with some certainty that what we have is only a fragment of what he intended to write, and that is one reason that later medieval writers attempted to make additions to the work. Some of these are interesting, though none has stood the test of time as Chaucer's tales have done. But of the 120 tales Chaucer planned to write, only 24 have come down to us, not all of them complete. Some, like the tales which the Knight and the Second Nun tell, he had almost certainly written a version of years before he decided to make a collection, probably with a particular event or celebration in mind, and it is all but certain that he revised some of these when he included them. We know that, in the fifteenth century, the work was very popular: 83 manuscripts are known, and of these 53 were intended to be complete, and this second group has been examined and catalogued, most recently by M. C. Seymour in volume 2 of his *Catalogue of Chaucer Manuscripts*.[1] Though there are textual problems here and there throughout the work which we now call the *Canterbury Tales*, it is certainly possible to believe that the medieval reader could indeed read Chaucer with evident pleasure and real understanding, and that, *pace* deconstruction, we can as well.

The most interesting thing about the *General Prologue* to the *Canterbury Tales* has to do with the *kinds* of characterization which Chaucer employs, the differences not only among the characters themselves, but how they are presented. It used to be thought that the *General Prologue* represented the author's remembered experience, and that the *Canterbury Tales* depicted a "typical" pilgrimage. In fact, this great if unfinished work presents a contrast, and sometimes a sharp one, within many of the characters, between the ideal and the actual, between their estate, or their social position, or their occupation and the equally constructed person whom he or she appears to represent, the person who may indeed take his or her identity from his or her estate, but who often pushes against that role, or evades it. Particularly in moments of confrontation, the tension between these oppositions reaches out beyond the *General Prologue* and into the tales themselves.

Probably when a student begins to read the *Canterbury Tales* his or her first inclination will be to ignore, or at least to avoid, the "ideal" or the "paradigmatic" in each of the pilgrims, and to focus on the "real" instead. This may be particularly true in the case of pilgrims who seem to present a vivid personality, like the Wife of Bath. But as a general rule, the pilgrims can indeed seem "other" to us, as much because of the way Chaucer constructs them as for their antiquity, and it is not surprising that, in writing or thinking about them, many students seek to turn them into characters from novels, to make them more modern, more "realistic," than they are. But this has also been the practice of earlier generations of Chaucer critics, who have sometimes either looked for original models for the pilgrims, or taken certain of them as personal or institutional targets of Chaucerian satire.

It is thus not always easy to know how to read Chaucer, whose fascination with detail and motive suggests that in some ways he was indeed a realist. But he stands apart from the nineteenth- and twentieth-century tradition of literary realism in which very many of the novels read in college and university courses, and about 80 percent of the novels published today, are steeped. One effect of having read such books can be to make a student miss the extent to which Chaucer was concerned with types as well as with persons, and also to underestimate the extent to which a pilgrim's social role figured in his or her composition. It is probably worth mentioning too that it cannot be assumed that the ideals which most of the pilgrims reveal, or to which they aspire, are necessarily "good." Most students of Chaucer have understood this in the case of pilgrims like the Pardoner and the Summoner, but have been more reluctant to concede that the office as well as the person of apparently more noble pilgrims, like the Knight, the Man of Law, or the Franklin, may also be subject to Chaucerian scrutiny, even though they may appear to be personally less "bad" than other pilgrims. The result of such critical practices has been to "blame" the person more than the office, and to think of Chaucer as more personally judgmental (damning the Parson and the Summoner to an Augustinian hell, for example) than reflective about what the pilgrims' social roles and responsibilities either are or should be.

The classic case is that of the first pilgrim whom Chaucer introduces to his audience, the Knight, to whose important, all-embracing person and tale I shall return in no less than three of the chapters. His tale is so powerful, so impressive, that a beginning reader almost needs to be warned about it. Indeed it is not beyond critical ingenuity to claim that almost any of the tales which follow have some sort of relationship to it – and in one way or another many of them do. In 1981 Judson Allen and Theresa Moritz published *A Distinction of Stories*[2] which argued, among other things, that the *Knight's Tale* was virtually the key to all of the major themes in the *Canterbury Tales*, so much so that virtually all of the other tales were reflected there. Other critics have been more circumspect, but the concerns of the *Knight's Tale* are often sounded in one context or another. No less problematic is its teller, who equally seeks to guide all who stand in his path. From the moment he appears he seems to be, as Chaucer calls him, without apparent irony, "a worthy man." He is described as loving the conventional components of chivalry: integrity and generosity, reputation and manners. He has fought in a long list of battles (too long a list to be taken at face value), and is said always to have behaved with courage and ability. We are told that he has "fought for our faith," and when engaged in one-on-one combat, he has "always slain his foe." Still, he is also represented as worthy and wise, "and in his manner as meek as a maid." He rides a good horse, simply decked out, and is modestly dressed himself, though his garments are coarse and his armor stained with rust.

More than twenty years ago Terry Jones, a very able medievalist who worked with Monty Python in *The Quest for the Holy Grail*, published what seemed at the time (and to many readers, still does) an outrageous but very interesting book called *Chaucer's Knight: Portrait of a Medieval Mercenary*,[3] in which he argued that Chaucer had portrayed a quite typical mercenary, who followed a career whose hallmarks were killing and power, but still claimed to be a follower of traditional knightly ways. Some details of Jones's argument were subsequently questioned or at least thought to be unproved: for example, when Chaucer says that the knight would "ride out," there is no particular reason to believe the assertion that this is a technical term indicating raids by members of a feudal army intended to loot from those through whose lands the army was passing; it probably simply means to go on expeditions, which certainly fits the context better. Equally, when Chaucer praises the Knight for his behavior in "his lord's war," he may not have been indicating any particular war of King Edward III's, but, as John Pratt insisted,[4] he may have been simply pointing to the Knight's traditional respect for military indenture. His appropriately small retinue may indicate his modesty, though it was quite usual in his period, as was his old-fashioned, but still praiseworthy, inclination to go on pilgrimage soon after his return to England. From the first, he appears to be one of us not only because he is a Christian, but also because with all his faults or with none, he is certainly very English.

And yet for all of these caveats, there is no more ambiguously noble a representation in all literature of a man whose job it is to kill people for a living than the one with which the *Canterbury Tales* begins, and Jones's funny but serious book really shook things up when he wrote it. Earlier suggestions that the Knight was not all he was cracked up to be had never gone this far, or been argued as passionately. Some of his points were subsequently called into question, but the issues he raised could not be easily brushed aside, and Chaucer's Knight would never look quite the same again.

More typically, in 1958, a very eminent Chaucerian scholar, E. Talbot Donaldson, had insisted in his edition of Chaucer that the names of the battles in which the Knight had fought "must have had for the contemporary reader the same proud ring that such names as Normandy, El Alamein, and Iwo Jima have today – great battles which momentarily united much of the civilized world against a common enemy." Donaldson's high praise of the Knight, which relatively few Chaucerians would endorse uncritically today, shows among other things how even "objective" readings of a 600-year-old text can be influenced by circumstances of the moment. In 1958, the World War II battles to which Donaldson referred were indeed widely known, and the sense of a common battle against sinister forces seemed a reasonable way to view the Knight.

Our own experience, on the other hand, in the intervening half-century, has been very different. We are now very quick to recognize that high ideals do not always last very long in battle, and that the military prosecution of even a noble cause usually carries with it unintended effects. Death by "friendly fire," by misadventure, by bombing error, are bad enough, but add to these the rapes, massacres, and simple murders ("fragging," in which a fragmentation grenade was tossed into the tent of a sleeping American officer when his men had no use for him, in Vietnam) which come with war of any sort, and we can see that the representation of the Knight in the *General Prologue* was more complex than scholars used to think, and probably represents a serious and complex meditation on the problems of chivalry, and perhaps on those of warfare itself. The Knight may be a good man living up to his ideals, but what if those ideals are flawed? No wonder as perceptive a critic as Lee Patterson, writing in *Chaucer and the Subject of History*,[5] could read in his tale, as in chivalry generally, "a failure of self-understanding" (227). In one sense, of course, there is no self to be thus misunderstood, but in another it is not difficult to see what Patterson is referring to. In the context of heroism, the Knight at first appears to represent the very center of the *Canterbury Tales*, a center which will supply a needed ideal, and define, in terms of that ideal, who is "other." But the profession which he follows has its requirements and reputation too, so that his is a center which, whatever this Knight's apparent motivation or idealized esteem, is finally defined by power.

Set this depiction of the Knight against the powerfully idealized representation of the parish priest, whom Chaucer calls the Parson. Throughout, there is really nothing in his attitudes, his behavior, or his values to which Chaucer takes exception, a simply extraordinary state of affairs, given the trenchant ecclesiastical satire Chaucer reserves for many of the other pilgrims, both in their descriptions and in their tales. That may explain why in the past he was associated with John Wyclif (c.1329–84), a Fellow of Merton College, Oxford, who preached a kind of radical (and needed) church reform which gradually metamorphosed into what was subsequently called heresy. The Parson himself is no Wycliffite (or Lollard, as the followers of Wyclif were often called), if for no other reason than he is on the pilgrimage, which followers of Wyclif avoided as immoral, and not leading toward the kind of biblically-based spirituality which they sought. But the terms in which Chaucer both describes and praises the man suggests a sympathy toward some of the church reforms which Wyclif himself propounded, and with which, before the 1382 ecclesiastical crackdown following the 1381 "Peasants'" Revolt, many agreed. There are few more controversial statements in this little book than the one I have just made.[6]

The Parson is described from the beginning as being "rich" in holy thought and work, a learned man, who would preach Christ's gospel truly, but who was concerned deeply for the poor in his parish, whom he served unstintingly. The figure of an ideal parish priest thus deeply informed his composition, and Chaucer assigns him a "wide" English country parish, almost as though it is England itself, with houses far apart, and notes that in time of need he would visit any of them, rich or poor, whatever the weather, "upon his feet, and in his hand a staff." He was a true pastor, not at all one of those parish priests whom Chaucer indicts, men who would leave their parish in charge of a curate and go to London, there to make good money by becoming a chantry priest, praying and saying daily mass for the soul of some rich man who had dedicated money for the purpose. But we must be careful not to take Chaucer's condemnations simply, or even as representing the way things were. In practice, the role of the chantry priest was often complex, depending upon the number of priests involved, and the nature of services expected of him. His duties could begin when the rich man in question was still alive and could attend to details, and particularly in cities like London, these details could involve a whole "college" of such priests, which would have assigned to it a variety of duties, including educational ones. Theologically, the whole operation, though orthodox, was more than a little suspect, since it seemed to some of those who endowed chantries to turn on the proposition that if they paid the priests for enough masses for them and for them alone (though sometimes for their families as well), they could thus negotiate, if not actually buy, their way into heaven. It is somehow typical of Chaucer, however, that he attends not to the motivation of the benefactors, but to that of the priests who cooperated in the arrangements – or in this case to one who did not. "He was a shepherd, not a mercenary," Chaucer drops of his Parson.

Still, Chaucer does not represent this ideal Parson as all things to all men. Devout himself, he did not snub or condescend to sinful men, whom he seeks to influence by kindness and fairness, though he was not slow to remonstrate with the obstinate, whether they be rich or poor. In all he did, he taught Christ's teaching and that of the twelve apostles, Chaucer concludes, "but first he followed it himself."

The description sounds on the face of it so straightforward that we pause a moment before realizing that it is deeply idealized, even while it is also exactly right to represent the perfection of religion in the *Canterbury Tales*, and in Chaucer. Turning from the church's spirituality to the mechanics of its operation, Chaucer then presents very different portraits of two ecclesiastical functionaries who ride together as "friends," the Summoner and the Pardoner. A "summoner" was a minor church official whose office it was to notify persons who have been called to appear before the archdeacon's court. Since it was an ecclesiastical not a civil court which he served, he was in minor orders, but his office required no great learning, and Chaucer's Summoner is no exception to the rule. Much has been made of the moral laxity which has resulted in his deformed face, and in *Chaucer and the Medieval Sciences*[7] Walter Clyde Curry insists that his physical description is that of a leper, a state conditioned "by illicit association with women infected by it" (45). Yet it is both easy and usual to overstate the complications of his putative personality, and depths of his moral depravity. Chaucer indeed indicates (and indicts) his greed and licentiousness, but also takes note of his vanity and ignorance: for example, the character is represented as quoting Latin tags he has picked up in court without understanding what they mean, and in a strange sort of way the evil which both he and the Pardoner clearly represent can be attributed in no small part to their occupations as well as to their persons, though Chaucer is well aware of the ways the job and the man go together. The descriptions by themselves make this connection quite clear, though in the past it has been obscured by the idea, first put forward brilliantly by E. Talbot Donaldson in "Chaucer the Pilgrim," an often-reprinted[7] article, that the *General Prologue* gives evidence not of one Chaucer, but of two. This idea argues that Chaucer the Poet, the world-famous poet who wrote the *Canterbury Tales*, oversees all and understands everything about the characters he has invented, but Chaucer the Pilgrim, the man who is actually riding on the pilgrimage, is at once more innocent, and far more limited in his perceptions. It is he who naively fails to understand what the Summoner means in one case, and says of him "a better fellow men cannot find," in another. But such ignorance, if it actually exists in the terms Donaldson proposes, not only assigns guilt too freely, but makes the whole argument too personal; the sense that there is an argument which the author is posing gets lost in the process.

It is important to consider the Pardoner's office quite as much as his putative character. Like all pardoners, he is represented as having a designated area in which to ride, preaching in church and granting pardons for money received. There are few medieval offices better calculated to outrage the modern temper, but in the fourteenth century the man's activities seemed to make sense. Sin was absolved by the simple act of going to confession, but temporal punishment left on the soul required further satisfaction and had to be remitted by prayer, fasting, or acts of mercy, of which giving alms was one. Throughout this period, a large number of duties fell on the church which, in the twenty-first century are assigned to municipal authorities. The building and upkeep of certain roads, the establishment and maintenance of some hospitals, these duties and others, depending on time, place, and circumstance, might devolve upon one ecclesiastical authority or another. It seemed only sensible to cancel the temporal punishment left after confession of those who were willing to assist in these important matters, and an in-church sermon – collection following – seemed a reasonable way of seeing who might contribute.

But the difficulty with granting pardons in this way was that the office created for doing so was filled with pardoners. Contrary to all regulations the man sells relics, and in the minds of his audience Chaucer's Pardoner probably would, as John Manly pointed out in *Some New Light on Chaucer*,[8] have been associated with a specific pardoner (also from Rouncival) who was known for his deception, sale of fake relics, and what we might reasonably call his irregular habits. Chaucer may imply that his Pardoner is carrying on a homosexual affair with the Summoner (though both scholars and the evidence are divided on this issue), and he certainly shows that he loves to exploit the poor, a real crime in Chaucerian fiction. But as with the Summoner, there seems to be no ideal or perfect form to which the Pardoner can aspire. He cannot become a perfect Pardoner because in a way, with all of his corruptions, that is exactly what he is. His art is that of construction, and since both ideal and practice are equally representative of human failure, they cannot but lead to an all-consuming self-importance which, translated into personal terms, leads to sin. He does not escape culpability, but the Pardoner is also what his office has made him, Chaucer insists.

Even the superior, idealized but imperfect Prioress does better than they, but she too is represented as living at some distance from perfection, a state manifested in her easy contempt for the poor, which is represented by the fussy and extravagant way she attends to the care of her small dogs, who matter more to her than any social obligation. I shall return to the Prioress in a later chapter, and to what Chaucer has identified as her understanding of what constitutes the Other, which he represents as deeply and painfully rooted in religion. But the only pilgrim shown to live at ease with poverty is another idealized pilgrim, the Oxford student (the "Clerk of Oxford"), and though a certain amount of his polish comes off in his tale, he is as thin as his horse, and takes greater care of his books than he does of himself. Chaucer's famous last line in the Clerk's description ("And gladly would he learn, and gladly teach") is one of the most quoted in the *Canterbury Tales*. Less often cited are his other idealized virtues: his dedication to study, his prayers for those who have assisted him financially, his modest and pithy style, and the "high meaning" which he is said to reveal, though these things are his defining characteristics. It is difficult, having simply read the Clerk's description in the *General Prologue*, even to guess the sort of tale which he is likely to tell, though it is concerned at once with the distance between the real and the ideal, and with the construction of the poor as in some ways an Other. Still, when all is said and done it is difficult to escape the impression that a certain hardening of the Clerk's character has come about in the course of the development of the *Tales*.

This (sometimes imperfect) balance between the ideal and real is of help in understanding how Chaucer constructs characters who are not "realistic" or "modern" in the usual meaning of those words, but both alike and unlike the characters whom we encounter in more modern fictions. As I have noted, the tension this opposition creates, together with Chaucer's brilliant attention to detail and motive, can encourage the reader to find in them somewhat more realism than is often present. It may have another unintended effect as well. It can also suggest that, for all of the social nuance which his pilgrims display, Chaucer's own "position" about the social constructions among which he was living is all but unknowable, or worse, that he himself avoided serious discussion of it. In an important article[9] Alcuin Blamires takes up this issue, and focuses, among other things, upon the person and the implications of Chaucer's Reeve, the manager, collector of monies, and above all the overseer, of all work done on a farming manor which he rules and exploits for his own advantage. Blamires shows in detail how deeply this Reeve, like others of his estate, is associated with the injustices and the oppressions of the poor, and he associates these injustices and deprivations with the 1381 revolt. Other scholars had felt the force of the Reeve's self-serving and rapacious personality and practices before, but Blamires is really the first to show how attached they are to his position in the social order, and how his exploitation of working men like the Plowman identifies and defines a general, not simply a personal, corruption.

Not that the man is free of personal corruption: Chaucer repeatedly suggests that his oversight of the farm's livestock, grain and agricultural productions is totalizing, and that no one is ever able to catch him out in his dealings. Indeed, he is represented as so well informed about what everyone is up to that the manorial workers are afraid of him as of "the death" - and "the death" here almost certainly means the plague. The further implication is that he has done well, personally, at his lord's expense, and in this connection Blamires points out that he is said to know the "sleighte and covyne" (604), the "stratagems and conspiracies," of those whom he over-sees, and that the word "conspiracy," in particular, is very likely to have implications which suggest incipient revolution. If it does, this is an extraordinary indication that, about ten years after the 1381 rising, Chaucer can allude to its grievances, and do so not from the point of view of those who were oppressed, but by describing one particularly nasty cog in the wheel which exploited them.

Blamires, however, does not see it this way. For him, Chaucer has "capped" responsibility for the exploitation of the poor at the level of the Reeve (though he also includes the hapless Miller in his in-dictment), who is in the end nothing but a peasant foreman, and he insists that Chaucer will not allow responsibility for the exploitation which was inescapably part of the manorial system to extend up-wards, to pilgrims like the Franklin, Knight, or Man of Law, where it rightfully belongs. He calls this blaming of mid-level management "displacement of oppression," and he names his important article "Chaucer the Reactionary," so as to indicate the ideological position which he believes Chaucer has taken.

But it is not clear in what way the evil which the Reeve inflicts may be said to be "capped" with him. On the contrary, he is in many ways represented as a symptom, not a cause. Chaucer's trenchant description shows nothing more clearly than a sympathy for those whom the Reeve exploits. He does not present such persons simply as victims, however, but, in the person of the Plowman, represents them as empowered by a moral integrity and a social power quite unknown to the Reeve. The Plowman is not a measuring-stick against which to set other peasant yeomen, but a reminder of the power and integrity of those whom the Reeve and his masters cannot sub-vert. It is of course true, as Blamires rightly insists, that Chaucer is no democrat, no Marxist, and in arguing, as I am here, that he is more insightful into the sources and operation of oppression than is frequently allowed, I should not turn him into one. He would no more have joined the 1381 rising than would, for example, John Wyclif, if only because any client of John of Gaunt, one of the main

targets of those who joined the revolt, would represent only circumspectly sympathy of whatever sort for the conditions which led
to the rising. But as he shows repeatedly, Chaucer was not indiffer-
ent to oppression, and his world is above all a connected one, so that
his descriptions of the pilgrims lack neither complexity nor connection. It is simply no longer possible to read the Knight as heroic and
well-traveled, or the Franklin as admiring and avuncular. Their
isolations, blindnesses, and insularities are as important to their construction as their virtues. An interesting and related aspect of the
Reeve is the way in which his aristocratic aspirations, apparent in
his "full fair" dwelling shadowed by "green trees," serve to remind
Chaucer's audience of their own connection to events which were
not of many years distance, but which, by the late 1380s, were usually sounded only indirectly. It is hardly possible to believe that many
of those in his audience who recognized the wrongs attached to the
Reeve believed that they ended with the man himself, and although
Chaucer represented the wrongs of his masters with his usual cir-
cumspection (the Knight does not behead peasants, nor does the
Franklin burn their homes), he does so unmistakably and with con-
viction.

In "reading" the pilgrims, then, it is important to notice how the
implications of their estates, no less than their apparent attitudes,
inform Chaucer's text. It is not difficult to subject the *Canterbury
Tales* to a Marxist reading, but in doing so Chaucer's own position
will emerge as ambiguous, in spite of, or perhaps because of, his
own occupations when not writing poetry. When the offices of the
religious are taken into account – Blamires points out that the "displacement of oppression ... operates in the [General] Prologue to
offload resentment on to religious practitioners" – together with the
shifting role of class, it is difficult to believe that Chaucer finally
sympathizes with the powerful. He may not have thought ideologi-
cally, but he did indeed think, and even though in such matters as
race he was far from any modern position, he was able to articulate
such issues and contradictions as were present to him and to his
contemporaries in language which all (or most) could understand.
To many of them, the peasant pilgrims were indeed "Other," as distant from their interests as any king in Asia, but it is difficult to read
the *Canterbury Tales* in general, and representations of pilgrims like
the Reeve in particular, without being aware of a conflicted sense of

nationhood which runs through it, and against which pilgrim, narrative and poet occasionally collide. In this context the "Other" is itself conflicted, since it appears no longer according to class or (usually) according to race. But it raises too what seems to be a partial and incomplete insight toward which, at least on a philosophical level, Chaucer's understanding of the Other moves: that although the Other seems to be one of the ways through which we define who we are, the universally accepted distinction between "us" and "them" is finally mistaken, and the alien, even the infidel, is who I am. As we shall see, this insight rested uneasily upon attitudes toward race and class which were in many ways quite unreconstructed, and which most modern readers will reject. But the *Canterbury Tales* is in the end a poem as conflicted as it is powerful, and we should not allow this other understanding of the Other to escape.

This conflict is brilliantly illustrated in the person of Harry Bailey, the energetic "Host" of the Tabard Inn just outside London (in Southwark, which has now been incorporated into the city), from which the pilgrims set forth on the ride to Canterbury. It is he who draws the group together, who makes the collection of pilgrims one, and Barbara A. Hanawalt has pointed out[10] that Harry Bailey is really imposing on the whole group the usual "municipal rules for taverns and inns" (117), so extending his authority, but as importantly he is defining who is "us" and who is "Other."

In fact, there is a barely suppressed joke about Harry Bailey (and about all others, ahem, who write about Chaucer) which Chaucer has snuck in: by common agreement at the time that they set out, Harry Bailey has been appointed the judge of the tales, the one to decide who among them will get a free meal, paid for by all the others, in his Tabard Inn upon their return – a good deal for the innkeeper, needless to say! But as the pilgrimage goes along, it becomes clear, from the superficial and often silly remarks which he makes at the end of many of the tales, that Harry Bailey understands virtually none of them. And he's the judge! Let all critics of Chaucer's tales beware! But remember, too, that that fact does not make him any less a member of the group, one of "us," not an Other.

Not all of the Canterbury pilgrims get to tell their tales. The agreement which the pilgrims struck was that each one would tell two tales going to Canterbury, two tales coming back – but Chaucer died while his work was still in progress. Only 23 of the pilgrims narrate their tales, and no pilgrim (with the comic but important exception of Geoffrey Chaucer the pilgrim) tells more than one. So the *Canterbury Tales* is a great but unfinished work, even though there is no work in English, Shakespeare included, which has contributed as deeply to all subsequent narrative.

But throughout the sense of "Otherness" runs deep in the *Canterbury Tales*, and is by no means limited to the *General Prologue*. This "Other" exists outside of the closed world which Chaucer describes, and is in fact made up of those who, by their presence, but also by their ideals, attitudes and assumptions, challenge that world, and can neither be dismissed nor ignored, though they are curiously recognizable, as though they are in some way a part of, not apart from, those who confront them. They can also be celebrated, however, and that is what one tale tries to do. Thus, when the Knight's young son, the 20-year-old Squire, comes to tell his tale he does so with great brio, but without much restraint at all. It is set in the East, somewhere in the Mongol Empire, and involves among others Genghis Khan, about whom the Squire knows absolutely nothing except what he has read in fiction. No matter. He launches his tale eastward, to a land filled with brass horses, magic mirrors, rings, and swords – and the whole thing gets splendidly out of hand. In the nick of time, one of the other pilgrims, the Franklin, intervenes, cuts the tale short, commends the teller, and begins his own, which we will turn to very soon.

But in a strange way there is only a limited sense of the "Other" in the *Squire's Tale*. It is too much stereotypes and special effects, with English chivalry at the bottom of everything. We shed no tear when the Franklin interrupts him, and offers to tell another – but meaning a better – tale instead. Still, in some ways, then, the *Squire's Tale* indicates how "the Other" is sometimes treated in Chaucer, in which what seemed to be other is not other at all, but simply one of us, dressed differently. But there is a moment when the "Other" seems to mean something else altogether, and that is when the number of pilgrims suddenly expands, first to two, then back to one again. Toward the very end of the pilgrimage, when the steeple of Canterbury cathedral seems almost in view, two men, a Canon in minor orders who turns out to be an alchemist, and his servant-yeoman, come galloping up – others indeed – and ask to join the group. On the face of it, this is an unusual request, since they are but five miles from the safety of Canterbury, and, in a moment of brilliantly con- ceived medieval "realism," Harry Bailey smells a rat. In a time when class distinctions seemed to be set in stone (but were also gradually weakening as well) he is almost familiar, and addresses not the Canon-Alchemist, but his servant, doing so in familiar terms, almost as if they were social equals. He begins by reaching out (or down) to him by calling him "Friend," and in spite of the greeting "Sir," which the servant-yeoman returns, there seems to be no apparent conde- scension in Harry Bailey's address. He continues with polite ques- tions, as to an equal, asking about the character and position of the Canon, digging deeper each minute, but simple and even courteous in his address. Caught off guard by such unaccustomed courtesy the servant melts, and offers to reveal everything. Hearing this, the Canon first calls a warning and then bolts, spurring away from the group he has just sought to join. Struck by his behavior and by Harry Bai- ley's confidence the servant then unburdens himself, and in the course of his tale reveals all of their alchemical secrets. Here too what seemed to be other – whether the galloping travelers or the pseudo-science of alchemy itself – is revealed to be only another aspect of what is already known.

Alchemy, the science which seeks to change base metals like lead into silver or gold, is a strange enough field of study by itself, but the Canon has practiced it in no small part as a way to cheat the gullible, hiding bits of gold in his mixture, and then, like a modern scientist falsifying his results to capture a government grant, extracting money from his clients so as to continue his dubiously useful work. Chaucer shows a degree of real interest in alchemy, though as the tale goes on he distances himself from it too, suggesting, in his own voice not the yeoman's, that it inquires into secrets of Nature which Christ will reveal only to those whom he wishes thus to instruct. But as the tale develops, its "teaching" seems to retreat into a world view which its action implicitly calls into question. There is something quietly subversive about this tale, which seems on the one hand to argue that scientific experimentation is a vain illusion which leads nowhere, but on the other that it ever drives people – or at least men – on and on, though not necessarily in their own best interests. Alchemy was an exception to the apparent medieval respect for all authority, so much so that it is sometimes credited with giving birth to the development of experimental science in general, and to chemistry in particular, while at the same time retarding their development in a naive search for silver and gold. In the end, the tale reaches out toward an "Otherness" which it cannot define, finally offering a profession of faith which makes the Other ours.

There are two other tales which, in different degrees, also explore the idea of Otherness, and they are the two tales told by Geoffrey Chaucer himself, the first of which is a parody, the second an allegory. The first begins as another Chaucerian joke. Chaucer tells a brilliant parody of the popular romances of his day, romances which often turned on the presence of giants, fairy queens, and wandering knights. His wandering knight is called Sir Thopas, and he really is a dud. He dresses elaborately, in all the latest styles, is said to be good at archery and wrestling, neither of which activities were expected of a knight, and he is certainly no lover. "Many a maid, beautiful in her bedroom, wishes for him as her lover," Chaucer remarks, "when she would do better to sleep." The reasons for his inattention soon become clear: he was chaste (no lecher, Chaucer brightly puts in), and he soon resolves (as the result of a dream) only to take a fairy queen as his lover – his own ironic idea of what constitutes the Other. Finally he sets out on his knightly quest, bravely riding through forests full of deer and rabbits, but then he finally meets a huge giant, Sir Elephant, who warns him to leave, since he has entered the land of a fairy queen. But this is just what Sir Thopas has been hoping for, and he warns the giant that he will taste his lance in the morning when he returns. The giant holds him in no great regard, however, and instead of lifting his spear, uses his slingshot to shoot some stones at him, but "with God's grace" Sir Thopas escapes, and gallops back to town to rearm himself. Before doing so, however, he decides to have a feast, and first the food, then the armor, is described at great (and comic) length, but by now Harry Bailey has had enough, and stopping Chaucer the storyteller in his tracks, demands another tale altogether.

This is of course part of the joke, that Geoffrey Chaucer, the greatest storyteller in the land, is prevented from telling his tale because it is so boring, though in fact is nothing of the sort, and the real difficulty is that Harry Bailey cannot tell a good parody (about other romances of his day, in this case) when he hears one. But Chaucer takes his interruption very mildly indeed and agrees to tell another tale instead.

This time he tells an allegory, translated from a French text which was itself translated from a Latin source, *A Book of Consolation and Council* (the title of the French translation was the *Le livre de Melibee et Prudence*), written by Albertanus of Brescia for his son in 1246. If the difficulty with Chaucer's first tale was that it had too little meaning, this one has little else but, though that does not prevent a certain fascination from developing. It sounds many themes, but the central narrative concerns an allegory about a powerful rich young man called Melibee, whose house was broken into by three burglars, who are named as the World, the Flesh, and the Devil. During their attack these three "adversaries" mortally wound Melibee's daughter, Sophia (the name means wisdom), and attack Melibee's wife, Dame Prudence. The three are then captured, and brought to Melibee for judgment. The question the tale brilliantly addresses is whether Melibee should take revenge.

His initial instinct is to do so, and since the implication in the tale is that he has the powers of a king, the tale addresses political as well as personal issues. Urged on by his wife and others, however, Melibee finally decides not to kill the burglars, but simply to impose a fine on them instead. Upon reflection, however, and after taking counsel of Prudence, he resolves even to forgo this mild punishment, and draws the three, who have cast themselves on his mercy, up from the ground on which they have been kneeling, thus forgiving them all.

The *Tale of Melibee*, as it is called, is something of an acquired taste, and there are some readers of Chaucer who either read it quickly, or not at all, and so may not find the interpretation I am going to propose very attractive. But depending on how it is read, it can also be viewed as one of the more proto-modern of Chaucer's tales, one which runs counter to an equally ingrained sense of Otherness, but which touches something compelling in his thinking and in his art. What Melibee has to face is his own participation in wrongs which he would prefer to think of as having been done *to* him, as Other than he. But this is no *Squire's Tale*, and those whom he confronts seem indeed to be Other, even though they lack the trappings of the East. After World War II the German philosopher Karl Jaspers published a short book called *The Question of German Guilt*,[11] which sought to consider, philosophically, who was responsible for the war which had just ended. Jaspers did not neglect the actual and immediate guilt of those who began and prosecuted the war, and also that of those who, even indirectly, supported them. But he also raised the issue of metaphysical guilt, of a kind of participation in the horror of war which emerges by virtue of being human, and so connects with all persons, German or not. "There exists a solidarity among men as human beings that makes each co-responsible for every wrong and every injustice in the world," Jaspers wrote, "especially for crimes committed in his presence or with his knowledge. If I fail to do whatever I can to prevent them, I too am guilty" (32).

This is indeed a challenge to most concepts of the Other, including medieval, but changes having been made, it is certainly present in this extraordinary tale. In some sense, this question of metaphysical guilt is one of the issues which the *Tale of Melibee* confronts, and the issue with which Melibee himself, with the assistance of Prudence, comes to terms. What he comes to understand is that the World, the Flesh, and the Devil are, in some sense, extensions of his own sinfulness; they are inner, not outward enemies. If he is to defeat these "adversaries" he can only do so by recognizing his own participation in their actions, and, in forgiving them, to renovate himself. The tale encodes also the Christian teaching of Original Sin, the concept that there is a kind of sinfulness which, since the time of Adam, and because of Adam's sin, all persons share. But Melibee's sin is not only Original and metaphysical: the sins which concern him, both immediately and finally, are also actual. After all, in everything but name, he is a king, and his so-called adversaries live in a world of his making. In this respect, the social implications of this tale are not very far distant from one encoded in a saying current among supporters in racial integration in 1960s America, "We have met the enemy and he is us." In the *Tale of Melibee*, perhaps exceptionally in Chaucer's tales, others are finally revealed as not truly Other, but an extension of myself.

If the first tale which Chaucer tells parodies the idea that art is, as in the *Squire's Tale*, a response to the exotic, his second shows that what is really foreign to us, what is really "Other," are the values upon which we construct our lives. In a work which gets much of its energy from a series of tit-for-tat dialogues between and among the pilgrims, the *Tale of Melibee* stands out less for its apparent allegory (Prudence gives birth to Wisdom, etc.) than for the radical nature of the proposition it advances. The sentiment in the tale was by no means unique in Chaucer's age, any more than it is in ours, and embraces too the author's desire to provide both pleasure and mean-

ing. But it offers a radically different, though theologically orthodox, way of articulating the concept of the Other, one from which
Chaucer himself in certain of his tales, sometimes shrank. As we
shall see, elsewhere Chaucer could be as insensitive as any modern
to those who were truly unlike him.

This concept of the Other is not, or not only, a modern and an
academic concern, but one which resonates throughout Chaucer's
culture, and which left many traces in the artistic, historical and
literary record of the period. Ruth Mellinkoff's great two-volume
study *Outcasts: Signs of Otherness in Northern European Art of the Later
Middle Ages*[12] treats, among other things, the many physical signs in
art and in life by which those who were seen as "other" were identified in late medieval England, Jews in particular (I, 100ff.). Indeed,
in one way in particular the identification of Jews in England differed from like signs on the continent, and was, in the end, particularly revealing. In England, the Tables of the Law, rounded,
diptych-shaped tablets well-known in European art, were used both
in art as an admired attribute of Moses, and, attached to clothing, as
an emblem to label and denigrate unconverted Jews. That the Tables of the Law which Christ had come to fulfill should receive such
ambiguous recognition is not inherently surprising, but it can suggest not only the ubiquity but also the depth of signs and attributes
which were deployed, in England as elsewhere, to keep the Other
away.

In the end, the sense of the Other in Chaucer's *Canterbury Tales* is
doubly constructed. On one hand, it is rooted in religious and cultural identity, in a sense which the late Ayatollah Khomeini articulated when he declared that "There are no frontiers in Islam,"
meaning that religious identity, in his case Islamic, takes precedence
over that of any nation-state. This sense is not absent in Chaucer,
who represents the slaughter of Muslims and Jews in contexts which
suggest at once approval and a real artistic failure, but it is complicated by another sense, in which the clear definition between "us"
and "them" is negotiated, even denied. Religious and national identity gives way to something even more pressing, an awareness of
self not predicated on the existence of others to give it birth or to
sustain it. This realization complicated but did not deny the sense of
the Other born of religious or national identity, or of class, and it
proved particularly powerful when certain of the pilgrims attested

to their faith. Christianity did not take as easily as Islam did to the presence of others around it, and this sense of the Other runs like an undercurrent throughout the *Canterbury Tales*, defining its objectives and complicating its effects. But it did not stop there.

I have been pursuing two themes in this chapter, the opposition of the ideal and the real, and the very medieval irony which that opposition can create, and the construction of the Other, a construction which Chaucer negotiates, and which is not the same in every place. Although it is not beyond critical ingenuity to suggest that these two concerns are connected – for example, by considering the ways in which the ideal is ever Other, or the ways in which the construction of the Other involves the operation of one or more ideals which the poet either embraces or rejects – in some ways they are irretrievably different, and speak as much to the agenda which the reader brings to the table as to any concerns in Chaucer. Yet the informing influence of the ideal is finally aesthetic, whatever its political implications; the role of the Other speaks first of all to an unacknowledged representation of difference, and although it has aesthetic implications as well, it does not lack political and cultural ones. No student of Chaucer can ignore either, since separately or together they help to identify a sense of recognition and wonder which any reading of the *Canterbury Tales*. Still, there are other, less attractive attitudes which lie beneath the surface of this great work. For all of the pleasure which it brings, the world of the Canterbury pilgrims is a foreign country, a place where they do things differently. And that is certainly a good place to begin.

4

Love

In order to understand the ways in which Chaucer thought about love it is useful to see how Chaucerian criticism developed in the twentieth century. For better or worse, it all started with a perceptive, multitalented, reputedly self-regarding, and really quite brilliant Harvard Professor named George Lyman Kittredge. In 1915 Kittredge published a book called *Chaucer and his Poetry*,[1] which changed forever the way we read the *Canterbury Tales*. It is not exactly true that nobody had noticed how closely some of the tales are tied to their teller before, but no one had looked as closely or as systematically as Kittredge did: and it is he who is credited with one of the earliest important insights into the way the tales are constructed, the development of what he called the "Marriage Group."

Looking closely, what Kittredge saw was that certain of the tales, those of the Clerk, the Merchant and, perhaps indirectly at least, the Franklin, refer to, and group themselves around, a strangely powerful character whom Chaucer called, with irony, the Wife of Bath. Alice of Bath is a clothmaker, an increasingly important trade in fourteenth-century England, and nobody's fool. In spite of her putative name she is nobody's wife, either, which is more to the point. Kittredge then proposed that certain tales respond to the challenge which the Wife of Bath has thrown down: "What is it that women most desire?" The answer the Wife of Bath proposed, Kittredge believed, was this: "Women desire to have sovereignty, over their husband as over their lover, and to be in mastery above them." Notice that Kittredge called the group of tales which depended upon that exchange the "Marriage Group," even though Chaucer alludes to

The Doctor of Physic (Hodnett No. 227)

lovers as much as to wives and husbands. But when the Clerk answers the Wife, he calls her by name, and it seems to be marriage,
not lovers, which concerns him. Look at it this way:

Wife of Bath: Five husbands and counting, besides other company in
youth.
The Clerk of Oxford: Unmarried, attentive to his studies, but also to others.
The Wife: Sits easily on an ambler. Has wide hips, with teeth set wide
apart. The sexual implications of this description would have been
obvious to Chaucer's audience.
The Clerk: His horse is as thin as a rake. He is too. The implications are not
sexual.
The Wife: Has been to Rome; to Cologne (to see the new gold shrine of
the Three Kings in Cologne Cathedral, which was still under construction
during Chaucer's lifetime); to St. James of Compostella, the end of a still-
active pilgrimage route in northern Spain; and to Boulogne in France.

Has experienced and enjoyed a certain amount of wandering by the way. *The Clerk*: Going to Canterbury, 54 miles from London. Rode down from Oxford to do so.

Kittredge saw all this, and more besides, and concluded that the tales had to be linked. And they were. At the end of his tale, the Clerk even refers to the Wife of Bath, praising her, even though he has told a tale which (he thinks) undercuts what she just said. But it hasn't, though (to him) it may have seemed to. Both, after all, tell tales about moral, devoted wives and unreasonable, demanding husbands, and in both cases the question of authority – of who's in charge – is central. Both begin with what amounts to a rape (though as the Clerk tells it, the father is informed beforehand, so it's legal), and both involve a passage of sorts, to seek an answer to the Wife's question on the one hand, and to endure the demands of an apparently fiendish husband, who could be taken to represent God (though there are other possibilities, too) on the other. But the Wife doesn't care. She's talking about something else entirely.

Kittredge then looked to the Merchant. He too refers to the Wife of Bath, or at least has one of the characters in his tale do so. The character even says she's spoken well, though he doesn't really think so. Still, the Merchant is deeply concerned with marriage, and at this point it's hard to say exactly what he thinks. An earlier generation of scholars even mooted the possibility that his tale was not originally intended for him at all, but for the Monk as an answer to the Knight, an answer more relevant than the one the Miller offers, because January is also a knight and loves the world of ideals. Certainly the wife in his tale, like Emily in the *Knight's Tale*, leads the dance, even convincing her (symbolically, but also actually) blind husband that the only reason he gets to see again at the end is because of what his wife has been doing up the pear tree with his young squire. "In he thrust," is the way Chaucer describes their tryst. But the teller to whom Chaucer first or finally assigned the tale, the Merchant, thinks marriage is a gyp, a total fraud. And he should know. He's been married all of two months.

Where was all this going, Kittredge asked? Not to the *Squire's Tale*, which comes next. It's too much a boy's book, and unfinished. The forceful Franklin interrupts him, won't let him disgrace himself any further. A real gent? But his tale is about marriage too, indeed it's about a marriage which really works, or so Kittredge thought. Better, the tale begins by bringing the marriage group itself to a close. The husband, Arveragus, is so much in love with his wife Dorigin that when he marries her he promises to assume no mastery over her, but only to claim sovereignty in name, since he is, after all, a knight, and has his social standing to consider. But then the Franklin seems to interrupt himself, and turn to the debate which Kittredge believed was raging around him. "Friends must obey each other," he insists. "Love will not be constrained by mastery. When mastery comes, the God or Love at once beats his wings, and farewell, he is gone. Love is as free as a spirit. Women, by nature, desire liberty, and not to be kept as slaves. And so do men, if I shall tell the truth."

Now look at the score, at least as Kittredge saw it:

The Wife of Bath: Women rule, except when they don't want to. Men should go along.
The Clerk of Oxford: God rules, usually through the husband, but the whole question is misdirected.
The Merchant: The whole question is not at all misdirected, and the Wife of Bath is right. Unfortunately.
The Franklin: Nobody's right. Trust = Freedom, and it's all leading up to a late Victorian view of marriage as the highest expression of love, which will culminate about 1917, when Kittredge will write his book.

It was such a powerful view that it lasted for decades, and it's not entirely gone even now, when scholars are more inclined to talk about the way love was constructed in courtly literature (avoiding the now dated term "courtly love"), than the ways it was articulated in late Victorian criticism, or experienced by living human beings. In spite of the way most of the characters in the group Kittredge identified refer to the Wife of Bath in and through their tales, relatively few critics still attach much weight to the marriage group, though fewer still fail to nod in its direction. But for many it has become a straightjacket, one which defines its topic too narrowly, and smacks too much of a nineteenth-century novel. Notice, for example, that when I wrote about the characters in the tale just now I wrote about them as though they were "real people" – which of course they aren't.

But there is another aspect of the Wife of Bath that the concept of the marriage group cannot address. For in matters of gender Chaucer is rarely if ever binary in his thinking, *pace* Professor Kittredge. He does not simply contrast women to men or men to women. Rather there are other categories which enter into the relationship, defining, undermining, or reformulating it, and the two primary ones, in Chaucer, are class and religion. Generations of Chaucer scholars have noted the importance of an emergent class consciousness in understanding the Wife of Bath, but many, at least, have treated it as somehow apart from her gender; in fact, it is how she registers her concerns with it. Even the religious knot in her tale, when one character tells another at a climactic moment, "Christ wills we claim our nobility of him," is a way of further defining and negotiating the issues of gender which have moved her from the first. In the same way, the *Second Nun's Tale*, a saint's life which is discussed in the next chapter, is deeply invested in women's spirituality, and so with issues of gender, which it examines in a largely religious (though also social) context. These concerns, together with such issues as class and religion, do not derail Chaucer's engagement with gender, rather they deepen it, and allow him to explore it in a social and cultural context which avoids simple opposites – good and bad, right and wrong – and to see instead the complicating and mitigating accommodations which, unlike Alice of Bath and St. Cecilia, many of his other characters observe.

Recently there have been a number of critical studies which have sought to broaden the terms of debate, and an important collection of essays on the *Wife of Bath's Tale* edited by Peter G. Beidler[2] takes up certain of these issues. The collection contains essays examining the tale from five perspectives – New Historicist, Marxist, Psychoanalytic, Deconstructive, and Feminist – and these readings, changes having been made, resonate elsewhere in Canterbury group. Taken together, they show the limitations of too static a reading, whether of the pilgrims or the tales, and the importance of acknowledging the presence of forces less personal than those which, in the past at least, have frequently engaged Chaucer criticism.

But Kittredge was writing out of a tradition of literary realism, and that was how *he* thought about narrative texts. To him, Chaucer's pilgrims were not very different from characters in, say, Dickens, so that it was quite natural for him to think of one pilgrim as responding to another's utterance. He assumed that his readership would share his assumptions, and until fairly recently it has. Although he responded to certain aspects of the Wife's subversion, he believed them balanced by the reactions of other pilgrims. But this analysis had the effect of so limiting the authority of any individual pilgrim's point of view that the only really omniscient viewpoint was the critic's. What Kittredge didn't see was how deeply subversive the *Wife of Bath's Tale* is, so that he became, like some later critics, so fascinated by the connections between and among the tales that it seemed to him that it was these which revealed what the tales really meant. The difficulty was that, in the exchange he discovered, the *Wife of Bath's Tale* became just one tale among many, and its obvious importance was diluted even as it was being acknowledged. In some ways, after all, it is Alice of Bath who calls the tune. It is her tale which sets the *Canterbury Tales* in motion, and her great themes, gender and class, which form the explosive mix which she holds out to Chaucer's audience, then as now. No noble woman, whether Constance in the *Man of Law's Tale* or Cecilia in the *Second Nun's Tale*, could speak as freely, or make the intellectual demands she does. Her class is integral less to her personality than to the way she speaks, though it also authorizes her experience, by which she attests to her gender, and accuses all men.

This was not, of course, how Kittredge saw things, though advance Chaucer studies he undoubtedly did. Thanks to his deeply representational way of reading fictions, he, and many Chaucerians after him, saw connections which had escaped earlier generations of readers. They emphasized the role and importance of the individual, the interplay between and among the pilgrims, the way one pilgrim "quits," or pays back, another for a real or imagined insult. Persons mattered, but so did class. In a way which Chaucer would have understood, the scholar's great strength was also his limitation. If everything is subversive then nothing really is, and the only solid surface is the one on which the Harvard professor stands. This had the effect of destabilizing the authority of the tale – and the author.

Interest in vernacular literary texts like Chaucer's *Canterbury Tales* gained particular strength after World War II when the study of English Literature came booming into the undergraduate curriculum, all but replacing Classics, and making authors who wrote in English the heart of the new syllabus. One of these was Geoffrey

Chaucer. Unsurprisingly, Kittredge's view of the pilgrims gained as-
cendancy. Its focus on the person, or as it developed upon the personality of the pilgrims, their interplay along the way to Canterbury,
and above all the way that they attacked and (sometimes) flattered
each other, opened new readings for virtually all of the tales, and in
succeeding decades Chaucerians developed a new reading of
Chaucer's masterwork.

Then in 1973 a young scholar in Cambridge reminded Americans
that they did not have a monopoly on Chaucer. In *Chaucer and Medieval Estates Satire*, Jill Mann proposed a new way of understanding
the way character is constructed in medieval texts, and in Chaucerian
texts in particular. The subtitle of her book, *The Literature of Social
Classes and the General Prologue to the Canterbury Tales*, showed the direction of her thinking. Characters were shown to represent, in dif-
fering degrees, the "estates," the occupations, professions and social
classes, to which they belonged. In a way already discussed, they
were not simply "individuals." This designation did not rob them of
their effectiveness, but it did provide a new way of estimating the
effects of the representation of character in the *Canterbury Tales* as a
whole. *Chaucer and Medieval Estates Satire*, though confined to the
General Prologue, located the sources for Chaucer's art not only in
history and person, but also in the secular and religious texts and
traditions he knew. It did not really interrogate the *Canterbury Tales*,
but it went beyond earlier source studies, some of them excellent in
their way, like J. Burke Severs's pathbreaking 1942 study *The Literary
Relations of Chaucer's Clerk's Tale*,[3] which sought to measure Chaucer's
originality by examining the ways in which, intentionally or not, he
changed his source, the book or books he had open before him, and
from which he translated many of his tales. Jill Mann's book sought
to examine the constructions which Chaucer found in his texts,
producing in the end a very medieval mixture of truth and poetry,
mimesis and poeisis. Markedly undogmatic, the book took Chaucer's
sources into account without losing sight either of his art or the
larger social constructions to which he was responding, and, to a
degree at least, creating. About ten years later, in 1983, an Oxford
scholar produced a book which read the whole of the *Canterbury
Tales* against this new evaluation. In *The Structure of the Canterbury
Tales* Helen Cooper moved beyond a new reading of character and
status in the *General Prologue*, and showed convincingly, and with

studied insight, that a less sentimental, indeed a less "realistic" reading, could also illuminate the great majority of Chaucer's tales, which now could be read as easily against each other, and within their immediate context, as against their tellers' preoccupations. Taken together, these two books prepared the way for the new reading of Chaucer, one which owed less to the pilgrim's personalities than to the tales themselves, which both authors saw as lively and interconnected.

A later chapter will take up Chaucer's complex view of death, a view which departs in many ways from both medieval and modern conventions, and is not concerned to show whether the tellers of the tales actually were talking to each other when they spoke. In the same way, it is possible to read the *Merchant's Tale* less as an embittered response to the Wife of Bath (though it is that too) than as a comic and sardonic retelling of a fabliaux, a type of tale which was intended for the nobility (or at least the upper classes), which, among other things, gave them an opportunity to laugh at their social inferiors. January may be a Knight, and his garden may carry both biblical and amatory associations, but the key which will open its door disarms any reading which is not at least partly comic. He also is an old man, a frequently recurring theme in the *Canterbury Tales*, written at a time in Chaucer's life when he may have been reflecting upon his own mortality. But, as Albert Hartung has pointed out,[4] in fashioning January Chaucer drew upon the late Classical poet Maximianus, a poet who, in the few texts of his which are preserved, often laments his lost youth, failed loves, and present old age, and who thus represents old men as objects of ridicule, not respect. January on his wedding night, credulous and foolish as ever, the slack skin about his neck shaking loosely as he approaches his young bride, stands for a kind of failure to understand experience which appears among old men in other Chaucerian fabliaux, and is often attached to amatory exploits which were better left undone. Chaucer's view of old age is finally somewhat conflicted, and though he was indeed able to represent it, dramatically in the *Second Nun's Tale* but elsewhere too, as worthy of reverence, he did not much esteem those among its membership who were either inclined to, or contemptuous of, human love.

But when we turn to the *Franklin's Tale* the importance of having another way of reading Chaucer becomes clear. For Kittredge, the

Franklin had in his tale more or less concluded the "marriage group," by preaching tolerance and forgiveness for everyone, though the powerful remained in power, which, in his somewhat Harvard view, was only as it should be. But the tale itself is otherwise. There is not much tolerance in it, and in any terms other than their own, the powerful have little to recommend them. Indeed, it is a tale almost calculated to outrage modern sentiment, and so read suggests that the somewhat sentimental reading of character often attached to the Franklin is probably mistaken. The almost studied insensitivity of a tale which reduces everything to a conventional construction of chivalry seems somehow altogether appropriate for this companion of the Man of Law (himself often a judge in the powerful court of assizes), former sheriff, auditor, and "knight of the shire," whose actual power seems so much sharper and harder than his fastidious tastes – or tale!

It is true, of course, that, as one expects from a man of his duties and station, his tale is deeply concerned with forgiveness, particularly of the sort needed to restore social stability. But why Dorigin needs to be forgiven is by no means clear. Her only fault, if you can call it that, is a devotion to her husband which leads her to agree to make love to a squire if only he will get rid of the rocks which she fears will wreck her husband's ship when, two years later, he finally returns to her. In fact, the squire does no such thing, but simply gets a magician to raise the sea so that the rocks will *appear* to be gone, and so offer no threat. Upon his return, her distressed husband seems more concerned for his good name than for his wife's, but agrees to the vow she has too hastily made (which prevents it from being a true vow, since true vows must be made only after due consideration, and freely) so long as his name is kept out of it, that is to say, she has to agree to tell *no one at all*. When the squire hears what has happened, and how Dorigin's husband has consented to her coming to the promised tryst, he in turn releases her from her promise, but is then himself forgiven the huge £1,000 fee he had promised the magician, who does not wish to seem less "generous" than everyone else. "Who is the most generous, the husband, wife, lover or magician?" the tale asks at the end.

Usually, any discomfort which the tale caused was blamed on the Franklin himself. Whether or not he is enamored of court customs, and is trying to distance himself from the functions he performs in the countryside and ingratiate himself with the Squire and Knight by reproducing in his tale what he understands only imperfectly, or whether, as Helen Cooper thought, it is a tale about virtue which indirectly echoes the *Squire's Tale*, which it follows, it is, as I have already suggested, an odd duck, like its teller, and curiously at war with itself. It has also seemed to me one of the more sexist of Chaucer's tales, though the *Reeve's Tale*, with its phallic delight in aggressive exploitation and its easy contempt for the naiveté of a working-class daughter, runs a close second. In a curious way it is indeed about love, though love of a particularly dependent and almost incestuous kind. The convention of the older husband and young lover (present also in the *Miller's Tale* and the *Merchant's Tale*) gets a new twist here, but whereas the other tales seemed somehow outside the conventions, what is repugnant about this one is that it remains within them. Thus:

Miller's Tale: Old husband, sexually active young wife, college student.
Merchant's Tale: ditto, ditto, squire.
Franklin's Tale: ditto, worried wife, ditto.

If the plot of each of these tales is similar, what makes them work is the changes, the exciting and added elements Chaucer introduced to – there's no better word for it – spin them in an unexpected direction. Again:

Miller's Tale: Chaucer adds Absolom, a second young man who is in minor orders, and also thinks he is in love with the lively young wife, Alison.
Merchant's Tale: An extraordinary conclusion, in which Pluto restores sight to an old husband so that he can see his wife making love, but Proserpina gives her an explanation which shows that really, he is still blind.
Franklin's Tale: A magician gives the squire the appearance of having fulfilled the wife's requirement, and produces other tricks besides.

These changes to the basic old husband–young wife–young lover plot, all point to the different ways – sentimental, "romantic," cynical, knowing – in which Chaucer treats love. In the *Miller's Tale*, for instance, the parish assistant or "clerk," one Absolom, falls for Alison, the wife of an old, but really well-meaning, carpenter. In such circumstances it is his "estate" which matters here, not his person. Like medieval readers, we are less interested in what he "thought" than what he was, though unlike most medieval authors, Chaucer has included a hint of a somewhat more modern concern for person, even (occasionally) for personality. But Chaucer's description shows Absolom to be fastidious and even prissy, squeamish too, when it comes to bodily functions like farting – though apparently not love-making. In a way this is to prepare us for the tale where farting has quite a prominent role, but Chaucer is also making fun of a literary convention which insisted that refined, well-mannered clerks set the standard for a love which seeks to gain the lady's favor. The belief was that they were far more suitable as lovers than most rough knights (like the one on the pilgrimage, perhaps, but unlike his son, the Squire) – and certainly millers and carpenters were no competition at all. That is why, in the tale, Absolom the fastidious clerk expects to have such an easy time of it with a carpenter's wife. He does not realize that a more modern clerk, clever Nicholas the Oxford student, has already popped in, and thinks him a fool. What Nicholas wants is quick sex, not deep love, and so does Alison. Only John, foolish old husband that he is, and Absolom, the self-deceived parish clerk, manifest the warm human virtue known as love, and they're yesterday's people. No wonder the *Miller's Tale* is such an effective answer to the Knight's.

Notice the utter lack of sentimentality and even a certain disdain for person which runs through all these tales. It is as though there is a hard shell to each of them, and then when you crack it, a hard inside, too. Status, and particularly social status, counts as much as anything – certainly as much as morality or personality, which in these tales hardly matter at all. The laughs which they encourage are not sympathetic. Like the good aristocrats for whom the tales were written, we laugh at the characters, not with them.

It is possible that the *Merchant's Tale* flirts with something greater, since Chaucer substituted Pluto and Proserpina, who appear at the tale's end, for Christ and St. Peter, who appear in other versions of the same story. Their presence keeps the reader reminded that the tale has an element of the joke in it, but it also makes the terms in which characters address each other suddenly more sophisticated, as if to prove that since love-making is no longer one and the same with love, it at least can be regulated. But the *Merchant's Tale* too has a hard exterior. Characters are a function of what they do, and we expect nothing very subtle from any of them, so that the best that they can do is to produce an ironic laugh. It is not an easy tale to sentimentalize.

Chaucer's addition to the *Franklin's Tale*, on the other hand, seems at first glance unlike either the Miller's tale or the Merchant's, introducing, in the person of a magician, a note of romance which seems at first sight strangely inappropriate in a tale so deeply invested in anxiety, guilt, and bargaining. But in fact medieval magic is a subject that is only now beginning to be understood, and in some ways it is the tone, not the feats, of Chaucer's magician which seems to be just right. Although much medieval magic either bordered on, or simply was, pure superstition (John the carpenter, the old husband in the *Miller's Tale*, practices the sort of invocation which only seemed to be religious, but really was magic), there was a great body of what was called "angelic magic" which derived from texts which sought to obtain visions which could lead to heavenly knowledge. Many of the most important of these are still virtually unknown, even to students of medieval religion, upon which the study of medieval magic impinges, though in 1998 Claire Fanger edited a collection of essays called *Conjuring Spirits: Texts and Traditions of Medieval Ritual Magic*,[5] which really did throw new light on the subject. It is not difficult to associate Chaucer's magician with the well-connected, powerful, and set-in-his-ways Franklin, but from another point of view he seems to be the kind of necromancer several contributors to Fanger's collection write about. He does not actually alter nature, though he does give the appearance of having done so, practicing a kind of "natural magic," an aspect of the astrology which interested Chaucer and many of his courtly contemporaries, and which they believed to be in no way contrary to the teachings of their religion. As Fanger's book shows, "angelic magic" rested on the authority of books, not experiments, and was calculated to lead to such ideals as the Beatific Vision, though one widely known text, the *Ars Notoria*, claimed descent from Solomon himself, and promised to lead its reader to such relatively innocent gifts as knowledge of rhetorical skills. Chaucer enlists ritual magic not as a love potion to change the lady's heart and move her to love (as was often represented), but more simply, as a support for one engaged in the quest for a lady's heart. It is almost as though in the *Franklin's Tale* love itself was not something magic could alter, a rare attitude in a medieval text, even if, in the mouth of the calculating Franklin, it is not particularly convincing.

But love is such a constant theme in Chaucer that there is hardly a tale in which it does not appear, and certainly there is no more powerful narrative than the Knight's, which turns again and again on the young knights' devotion to their unknown and unloving lady. In *Chaucer and the Subject of History*[6] Lee Patterson points to an article Charles Muscatine published in *Proceedings of the Modern Language Association* (*PMLA*) in 1950 as the beginning of a reading of the *Knight's Tale*, which stressed form and texture while seeing the tale itself as a "struggle between noble designs and chaos" (165). This very literary reading of the tale Patterson believes has been effectively challenged by critics from the right, such as D. W. Robertson and Bernard F. Huppé, who view virtually any abridgment of hierarchy as a sign of irredeemable moral failure, and from the left, like David Aers and Stephen Knight, who see Theseus as "a cruel tyrant," and the tale as an effective Chaucerian commentary on "the decline of medieval chivalry into brutal exploitation" (167). But this now familiar distinction does not reflect the larger patterns of consolation and disorder present in the working out of love in the *Knight's Tale*, and my last chapter, "Death," turns to the only more apparently radical disruption of dying, which runs throughout the tale, imparting a formal pattern to the narrative as a whole, in its totalizing way restoring the social constructions which love had shaken.

But death does so quite impersonally, and the constructions which Theseus hastily arranges around it as he invokes the First Mover to explain its presence hardly account for the shattering power of the loves we have seen throughout. Order restored is certainly an important aspect of the tale, although, as the second group of critics might contend, it is a constructed, not a natural order which is restored, the product, at least in its visible and effective parts, of humans, not gods. The young men in this tale operate in a kind of philosophical and emotional fog, at least until the end, when Arcite's knowledge that he is about to die, having at once both won and lost his lady, moves him to speak with greater depth and sentiment than he ever has before. This is the moment to which I shall return in a later chapter, but it is impossible to pass over such a powerful moment here too, when speaking about love. Dying, Arcite pauses to

"Declare one point, from all my sorrow's pain to you, my Lady, whom I love the most. I bequeath the service of my soul to you, more than to any other creature," he continues,

> "since my life must end. Alas the woe, alas the sharp pain that I have suffered, and for so long! Alas my death, alas my Emily! Alas my leaving of this company! Alas my heart's Queen! Alas, my wife! My heart's lady, my life's end! What is this world? What do men ask to have? Now with his love, now in his cold grave, alone, without any company! Fare well, my sweet foe, my Emily.

He then asks her to take him in her arms and pay particular attention to what he will say now, for now he is finally going to stop talking about himself, and recommend to her his antagonist and rival, concluding, "if ever you shall be a wife, forget not Palamon, this gentle man."

This is one of those very few moments in the *Canterbury Tales* in which, even as we recognize the literary and social constructions which make them up, Chaucer's characters seem to speak, if only for a moment, without metaphor, symbol, or allusion. It's nice to think so. In fact, the rhetorical gravity of the language, the studied, even contrived circumstances (which depend on Chaucer's source, Boccaccio's *Il Teseida*), the act of closure which the scene and the words together define, all indicate the nature of the construction, without, however, stripping them of their somewhat formalized power. Such scenes are not at all uncommon in Chaucer, but in a now famous article on "pite" in Chaucer, written for a collection of articles dedicated to the memory of J. R. R. Tolkien,[7] Douglas Gray, the scholar to whom I have dedicated this volume, points out the way in which a human quality like "pite" can reach out beyond the tale itself to involve the reader. Construction need not mean artificiality, still less hypocrisy. This is an important aspect of Arcite's dying, and another example appears when the Clerk answers the Wife of Bath, at least in part by describing what a genuinely loving marriage should be – though he does so after it has broken down, and the peasant wife, Griselda, is being turned out by her autocratic (and aristocratic) husband, Walter. She cannot receive back her dowry, she tells him, because she brought none except her cheap clothes, which are now long gone, but then suddenly she interrupts herself:

"O good God! How gentle and how kind you seemed in your words and your countenance the day we married," she tells him. "Love is not the same when it is old as when it was new, but certainly, my Lord, no adversity can ever make me repent, by word or deed, that I gave you my heart without any reservation." There are few more powerful expressions of love in Chaucer, who was inclined rather to treat love as a social construction into which, generally in time, human emotion could enter, but there are too moments which reflect studied construction and love's power at the same time, and the lines in the *Clerk's Tale* stand out as one of them, as poignant for the sense of love remembered as for the consciousness of present loss.

A third passage where Chaucer constructs the powerful reality of secular love appears in a by now familiar tale which begins with a rape and ends in bliss – the *Wife of Bath's Tale*. But as Chaucer developed the character of the Wife of Bath she emerged as in many ways the most polished and apparently most modern of the pilgrims. She was a woman with her own needs, drives, and conflicts, the first such to appear in English literature. She has indeed been through five husbands, three old, rich, and dead, who left her goodly inheritances, a fourth who (foolish man) kept a mistress, and whom she may have driven to an early grave. A fifth husband was young, sexy, and intellectual, and though he may have married her at least in part for her money, he found, like the others, that there was more to the bond than he put his hand to. His recent and unexplained death she much regrets, even though it has not kept her keeping an eye open for number six.

It is out of this background that the Wife of Bath tells her tale, really about the education of a young knight at the hands of the ladies of the court, who save him from execution for a rape he has committed by setting him on a quest to find out what it is "that women most desire." The ironic answer to the question, which the knight learns from an ugly old woman who extracts from him the promise to grant her whatever she asks of him, is "sovereignty," and the old woman, supported by the ladies of the court, requires of him his hand in marriage. His hand she gets, but little else besides, and when she upbraids him for his haughty standoffishness he explodes, revealing that it is the insult to his family name that he most regrets.

What follows is a complex scene, at once sentimental and socially conflicted, in which the old lady explains to the young knight that by itself old money is worthless, and that Christ demands that we claim our nobility from him, by reason of our "virtuous living." She then offers him a choice: she can remain as she is, but she will be true to him all her life, or he can have her young and beautiful – and take his chances. When he resigns the choice to her ("My lady, and my love and wife so dear, I put myself under your wise governance; choose yourself which may be most delightful, and do most honor to us both"), she lets him have the best of both worlds, that is, she will be both beautiful and true, unto his life's end.

This certainly is not the modern view of love, and not the medieval either, except in fiction. So what do these three lovers have in common, Arcite dying, Griselda driven from her home, the victorious, but apparently submissive, old wife, made young again? In his contribution to a 1998 anthology of essays *Love in Asian Art and Culture*[8] Hiroaki Sato noted that Japanese court poetry offered no parallel to the sort of physical lovemaking recorded elsewhere, but instead creates a world in which the joy of sex has been deliberately excluded. Though this is a circumstance not unknown to Western medievalists, the texts which interested Sato concern themselves with a longing for love, a longing which has been misunderstood, or as often misconstrued, sometimes deliberately so, but constructed so as to account for, if not finally to explain, the complex thing which love may be. This love of longing, constructed but attentive to the fact of love itself, is also present in Western medieval art, and in Chaucer, and for this reason, while it is indeed important not to assume that *all* Chaucer's attitudes toward love or toward anything else came as a result of his culture and his reading, it is equally important not to think of him as finally apart from his age, as our contemporary. Still, there is certainly something modern in the sense Chaucer conveys that love is most often seen fleetingly and in recollection, and that it is inseparable from the pain it causes or which gives it birth.

It is true that, in the *Knight's Tale*, Theseus can invoke "The God of Love" with the interjection "How mighty and how great a Lord is he!" But the deepest image of love, not only in that tale but also in all of Chaucer, appears on the walls of the temple of Venus in which Palamon prays – successfully, as it turns out. There is little in the disorder represented upon the walls to encourage him: sleepless nights, cold sighs, tears and lamentations first of all, and these followed by a litany of love's attributes: amusement and hope, desire and foolishness, beauty and youth, fun and money, seduction and rape, lies, flattery, much expense, attentiveness, and above all jealousy, wearing a garland of yellow marigolds, and holding in her hand a cuckoo, the symbol of infidelity. These are in turn surrounded by representations of dinner parties and dances, songs and many sorts of display, display of attraction and affection, "all the circumstances of love," Chaucer plainly says. Even Venus' own dwelling, with its pleasure garden around, has Idleness to open the door, and within are representations of Narcissus, who fell in love with his own image; Solomon, here remembered for his many wives; Hercules, whose great strength was overcome by infatuation; the witches Circe and Medea, who kept their lovers by magic; the hero Turnus, whose love led to his destruction by impelling him to fight an even greater hero, Aeneas; and rich Cresus, made a slave by love. What these all show, Chaucer remarks, is that wisdom and money, beauty and guile, strength and courage, are as nothing when set against love's really quite impersonal powers. But if love can indeed triumph over every human heart, it rarely brings happiness, even to those who most revere it. Rather, for Chaucer, love may be real, but it is also fleeting and disruptive. Its power, its effects, are everywhere, in delighted and in helpless lovers alike. On one hand, it rules the whole world, and all people respond to it; on the other, it settles nothing, and leaves only disorder and misery in its path.

The three lovers I have been talking about, Arcite, Griselda, and the old woman, each in some way deepens and clarifies Chaucer's view of love, which in time, and with changes having been made, fed the modern. Arcite, thrown from his horse to die just as his victory seemed complete, reminds even the bravest lover that he or she must die, that love will not outlast the grave, and that just when you think that you have mastered love, have finally gained control, really, you have done no such thing. I shall return to this most dramatic and powerful scene, one of the greatest in Chaucer's canon, in a later chapter, when I consider the role of death throughout Chaucer's tales. But it is not that Arcite's heroism, courage, strength, and valor count for nothing. They account for a great deal, having turned him from a youth into a man, having made him attractive as a lover, having given him a self-constructed reason to live the life he has. But in spite of everything, they have turned out to be dependent attributes, unable finally to stand alone, to see him beyond the grave, attached to a love which is not, as it happens, as strong as death. But as we shall see, Death is powerful and imposing, and stands, finally, above everything and everyone in the tale, but also apart from them as well.

Griselda, cast out of her home by an apparently unyielding husband and seeing the end of love, understands what Arcite cannot. For her, love lives in memory, in the altogether unmodern sense that, though old love is not like new, it still endures in her, if only in her refusal to believe that it was nothing. Her father is present, in some lines which Chaucer added to his source, to register the wrong that her husband has done her, cursing the day and hour that Nature gave him life, reflecting a view like that of Egeus, Theseus' father, who saw life as "a thoroughfare of woe," in which joy followed woe, but woe ever comes back again. In Griselda, however, Chaucer has created a kind of exception to the rule. For all of the echoes of religious love Griselda's tale encodes, her love resides in her integrity, and it is almost as though for a moment considerations of class, so important in her husband's apparent rejection of her, count for nothing. This is, of course a fairly formal (and constructed) attitude, and is present elsewhere in Chaucer, but deeds done, expressions of human love among them, can neither be forgotten nor suppressed, and in this sense, at least, love is indeed, as the psalmist says, as strong as death.

Finally, the old woman, whether a surrogate for the Wife of Bath or not, reminds us again that we are reading fiction, not fact. The very promise of truth and beauty is itself a warning, as something which even Nature can never grant. The quest which ended by bringing the young rapist, who happens to be a knight, to his knees, has this effect, that it reminds us, in spite of the woman's promise at the end, that whatever the human heart wishes cannot endure. Even sovereignty, once achieved, transforms itself, and the now-young woman becomes submissive to the one who has the least reason to deserve or expect it. But will it last? Nothing else in the tale has, whether the knight's apparent power or the court's authority. Even the other apparent link with the *Clerk's Tale*, an embedded concern for social class which thinks itself more powerful than love, vanishes beneath the woman's touch: it is not the knight's rape which betrays his class so much as it is his incomprehension of the ways in which his actions finally make him what he is. It is thus that he is reminded – or perhaps told for the first time in his life – that love is not something which comes automatically to someone with an old name or a lot of money. It is instead intimately caught up in who we are, and what we have become. The "sovereignty" which the knight comes to believe is what women most desire, is more than a mirror reflection of his own desire for power, manifested in the rape with which the tale begins. For this is a sovereignty which dissolves into submission, a submission predicated on the assumption that the partner will be true, and not make unreasonable claims. It is sometimes thought that the *Wife of Bath's Tale* ends in a romantic commonplace, and everyone lives happily ever after, but really they do no such thing. The implications of the tale may elude its sentimental teller, but as in all good fiction, they raise issues which continue after the narrative itself is over. We hesitate to ask if the young knight and the now-young lady live happily ever after, because text and prologue alike have taught us to distrust closure, particularly where love is concerned. Instead we readers permit them to hold out an ideal which is also a model for human happiness, but one which is rarely realized, at least in this world. Even in a tale like the Wife of Bath's which seems, of the three, the most irredeemably secular, the final effect is to look beyond the sensual moment in search, if not of a monument of unaging intellect, then at least of a land where soul can clap her hands and sing.

5

God

It is all but impossible to forget that, however secular Chaucer's pilgrims may appear to be, they are all on pilgrimage, and have, both physically and symbolically, one end in mind. Their pilgrimage is, among other things, a metaphor for the life of every Christian, indeed every human being. "Our hearts are restless until they rest in Thee," St. Augustine had insisted, and the finally unsatisfactory elements of any human life seemed, for many in the Middle Ages and after, reason to go on pilgrimage. But Chaucer's pilgrims never arrive. They are always en route to a destination where the arrival matters very much indeed, and for which their pilgrimage is only a prologue. An older school of Chaucerians laid claim to the mantle of Augustine, and were as willing as canon lawyers to condemn the sinful, reject mitigating circumstance, and pronounce definitively. But really nothing is settled. Chaucer constructs the pilgrims as knowing travelers, though their destination is barely in sight as their tales come to an end. They live somewhere between Babylon and Jerusalem, and turn sometimes to one, sometimes to the other. Their vacillation does not prevent them from asking, or at least implying, hard questions, but it should make us reluctant to offer easy answers. Hate and love, belief and doubt, coexist easily among them, and it is out of them that the religiousness that readers can attach to Chaucer emerges, and out of the realization of the place of sinfulness in human life.

This last concept is not particularly modern. Today we have many ways to account for aberrant behavior, psychological and sociological explanations among them. Still, it is important to remember that

The Wife of Bath (Hodnett No. 227)

the human realities which support these alternative explanations were present in the medieval period, and as such appear in many medieval texts, including Chaucer's. But the concept of sin runs throughout the *Canterbury Tales*, nowhere more impressively than in the *Parson's Tale*, a challenging text to read carefully. This tale approaches sin by fastening upon the choices all human beings are called upon to make, and attaching these choices to ecclesiastical ways of accounting for, and judging, the actions which follow – indeed, the work itself is a translation of Latin works, and one in particular, which are concerned with the causes of sin and contrition. The workings of sin and forgiveness were at once complicated and familiar in the fourteenth century, and elsewhere, as in his treatment of the Pardoner, Chaucer clearly expects his audience to be familiar with their operation, and in particular with the way in which once sin is forgiven temporal punishment remaining on the soul can only be removed by acts of satisfaction, such as prayer and almsgiving. But the *Parson's Tale* is, for Chaucer, a strangely psychological work, deeply invested not in the mechanics of contrition, confession, and satisfaction, but in the motivation for sin and repentance which lies behind them, and concerned too with what makes us behave as we do, with what makes us human. In a perceptive article[1] Thomas H. Bestul has set the tale against a late medieval tradition of religious meditation, and this is a particularly helpful perspective, if only because it prevents us from reducing the tale to a list of causes, or seeing it as a rejection of the art of literature, simply because the Parson insists he will not tell a fable.

The tale itself treats such topics as "the six causes which ought to move a man to contrition": remembrance of past sin; disdain of sin; dread of Doomsday; remembrance of lost goodness; remembrance of Christ's passion, and the hope of forgiveness; the gift of grace; and the glory of heaven. The tale also includes a detailed and splendid rendition of the Seven Deadly Sins – Pride, Envy, Anger, Sloth, Avarice, Gluttony, and Lust – attitudes and states of mind which, though not sins in themselves, lead the unwary Christian into sin. But what may be more important is the way in which the *Parson's Tale* provides a reflective, more than a moralizing, context for the lives we lead, and the attachments they may have to the life of the spirit. When the Parson warns against those preachers who, by rhymes, tales, and fables "adulterate the word of God," he is more than anything reminding his auditors that the spirit is separate from the world, that it is, and must be, in some sense Other, even though it equally attests to the power of grace and the love of God. Though not central to the tale, these theological constructions are present as assumptions and givens, and amount to what the Parson calls the "fruit of penance."

Like all Chaucer's tales, the surface of the *Parson's Tale* is only its beginning, and its powerful but narrow concerns do not define Christianity even when they assume what may have been one aspect of Chaucer's view of it. So understood, its attractiveness is at least partly aesthetic, bringing the collection of tales to a powerful and effective end and returning the audience to the world of fact and action. But it is also didactic, though in the end less admonitory than discursive, seeking more to awaken introspection than to impose morality. Given the Christian optimism in which it is grounded, it is in the end, as the Parson foretold, a "merry tale," one which will "show the way" to the celestial Jerusalem, and so engage that mixture of "sentence" and "solaas," of meaning and consolation, which the host placed before the pilgrims as the model for their tales while they were yet in his London inn.

But often we do not take for granted what Chaucer does. In the curiously aggressive but finally unconnected exchange between Summoner and Friar, religious issues are defined in the negative, by what they are not. Jokes abound: an off-color, but not too bad, story about the friars in hell who live like bees in Satan's arse; another about a summoner whose office is so like the Devil's that he expresses only mild surprise when he happens to encounter a demon on his travels ("I am a fiend; my dwelling is in hell." "Oh what say you? I thought you were a yeoman."). Indeed, the summoner at once joins forces with the demon, and hopes to teach him a trick or two. But the *Summoner's Tale* caps this with the tale of a friar whose fascination with the requirements of his office are such that, like a pedantic scholar, he seeks most of all to know how he is to divide a fart which has been presented to his convent.[2] All of these may be deformities of revealed religion, of Christianity turned inside out, but Chaucer implies that, whether they are or not, they are not at all uncommon, and are in fact the social constructions which have become integral to the ways in which Christianity is practiced and understood. He does not diminish these deformities; even his ridicule implies that they matter. Thus the *Summoner's Tale* begins with a friar's vision, but as a friar he is ravished to hell, not (as is usual in such visions) to heaven, since it is there that he is bent. The representation of the friar within the tale follows most of the more familiar constructions of friars: this one is at once deceitful and unctuous, and full of himself as well. In one particularly well-realized moment, he sweeps a cat off a bench where he is about to sit, a superb narrative detail which defines both the man and the moment. In the *Friar's Tale*, the summoner's nonchalance at meeting a demon in his travels acknowledges the thin line which separates this world from the next, and then plays with the danger of crossing it too easily. Both tales also play with the idea of pilgrimage: the friar in the *Summoner's Tale* travels to secure gain for himself and his convent, but his is not the spiritual end which pilgrimage presupposes. The summoner in the *Friar's Tale* equally rides less to perform his office than to win what he can.

But in the brilliantly retaliatory *Summoner's Tale*, the rapacious friar's love of learning indicts not just Christian learning, but any which separates itself from its final cause, and becomes, with however fine a flourish, an end in itself. It is finally the sins of the religious which matter most of all, but these sins encode their opposite, complexly arguing for what their agents most vehemently deny. In developing this exchange Chaucer turned, with a surprising depth of knowledge, to a tradition of anti-friar satire, documented by Penn R. Szittya in *The Antifraternal Tradition in Medieval Literature*.[3] As always, Chaucer manipulates the tradition he is working with, undermining its givens, and sometimes gleefully encouraging its excesses. The summoner may end his tale in an ironic Pentecost, but it is hard to say how far this raucous parody is intended to have any theological meaning. Except in modern America, the deformities which religion makes are as often funny as shocking, and only the most innocent will be impaled upon them.

Other religious difficulties are more lexical than comic. After a lengthy description of the Prioress in the *General Prologue*, Chaucer remarks simply that she had another nun with her, who served as her secretary, and "preestes thre," apparently "three priests." Early illustrations of the Canterbury pilgrims, like that of the great British artist, printer, and poet William Blake (1757–1827), dutifully show three priests riding along in the Prioress's wake, accompanying her and her companion nun, though evidently in a secondary position. No more. For reasons of syntax, style, and revision, the line is now read, "and a priest made three," that is, this was a group of three persons riding together as a party, which, for reasons I hope will become clear, I shall call the Prioress's Group. What makes the group particularly interesting is that it is the only group among the pilgrims all of whose members have taken religious vows, and it contains both the Prioress and her nun-companion, the "Second Nun," who together make up two of the three women pilgrims who tell tales (the third being the Wife of Bath). More importantly, the tales they tell are both intellectually provocative and subtly connected. Probably Chaucer would have lengthened his *General Prologue* descriptions of both the Second Nun and the priest who accompanies her and the Prioress (the "Nun's Priest") had he lived to do so, but as things stand he realized in their interplay an extraordinary discussion of the way religion works, and is seen to work, in the lives of everyday Christians. And the really unusual thing is that he begins the discussion with a tale which is un-mistakably racist.

Out of this extremely interesting group of three pilgrims and three tales emerges one question which links them, and which has not been previously addressed in the numerous allusions to the divine which have already appeared: How does the supernatural enter into human life? When is it that the text reflects not simply the abiding presence, but the actual entry of the supernatural into the lives of persons, an entry not predicated on human sinfulness, ecclesiastical constructions, or devout formulations? In this chapter and the next I shall argue that this question is neither academic nor naive, and that Chaucer's understanding of the divine develops through a kind of dialogue within a received tradition, in which one tale reflects upon the next, so that although the putative persons of the pilgrims are indeed involved, what is finally at stake is something greater, a serious reflection upon the ways in which God enters, and is per-ceived to have entered, into human affairs. After all, the under-standing and image of the supernatural which emerge in the tales responding to the Prioress differ in many ways from other tales in which God is indeed present, but present as an impending and ever-present power, not a being whose presence emerges as the tale de-velops. There is not in this group the clear assumption of a divine order manifested in a visible and regulating church, which under-lies the *Parson's Tale*. Nor is there the evident allegory of the *Clerk's Tale*, or the easy confidence in divine intervention of the *Man of Law's*.[4] These tales attend rather to the ways in which the super-natural enters the world, and while they insist upon faith in God's protective power, they do not disguise the necessity for human ac-tion, the uncertainty of divine intervention, or the difficulties and contradictions which faith can entail.

Thus God (but also God's opposite) enters the *Canterbury Tales* subtly, and in order to see the effects of supernatural intervention we must remain attentive both to what the characters do and say, and also to their attitudes and assumptions. We will then turn, in the next chapter, to the ways in which Chaucer moved from literary to sacred visions, using epistemology to grasp even as unmediated a meeting with the divine as visions were believed to reveal.

The Prioress, who initiates the discussion, begins by telling a tale which is at once virulently antisemitic and devoutly, but not deeply, religious. It is the tale of a seven-year-old Christian boy who lives in an unnamed Asian city, and who must walk through a Jewish ghetto on his way to school every day. Taught by a friend, he sings the "Alma redemptoris mater," a song in honor of the Blessed Virgin Mary, as he does so, outraging the Jews who, urged on by Satan, arrange for a murderer to cut his throat, and throw his body into the public sewer. His distraught mother, half out of her mind, seeks him everywhere, but without result, until the boy suddenly bursts into song, singing the "Alma redemptoris," which leads immediately to the discovery of his body. The Provost of the city orders all Jews "that knew of the murder" to be put to torture and shameful death, drawn by wild horses and then hung ("according to the law," the Prioress, or perhaps Chaucer, sanctimoniously adds). Meanwhile, the boy is taken to a priory where he lies before the high altar while a mass is said, after which he is sprinkled with holy water, which causes him to speak. Enjoined by the abbot to say why he is singing, the boy explains that Mary has placed a grain upon his tongue to enable him to do so, and when it is removed she will conduct him to paradise. The abbot removes the grain and the boy dies "full softly," an event which causes the abbot to fall face-down upon the ground and lie as one dead. The order thereupon carries away his bier, and entombs him in marble.

You don't have to live in the twenty-first century to recognize a cultural stereotype in all this. Antisemitism was the most widely spread, and most virulent, form of racism present in the Western Middle Ages, and it runs over in the *Prioress's Tale*. In *Gentile Tales*[5] Miri Rubin has written perceptively about the depth and range of medieval antisemitism, particularly as it relates to the many false accusations associated with the consecrated eucharistic host, and the same sense of bigoted moral outrage which informed the fictions Rubin discusses is present in the *Prioress's Tale* as well. Though there were no Jews in England at the time Chaucer lived (they had been expelled in 1295, about half a century before he was born), Chaucer had traveled often on the Continent (but not in Asia), and knew well enough the conditions under which many Jews were forced, by Christian authorities, to live. But what matters more than any tangential tie to history is the nature, but also the tone, of the spirituality which the Prioress preaches. The tale is nothing if not emotional, but it is also deeply sentimental. The supernatural enters with the miracle, signified by the grain which Mary places in the boy's mouth, and though there have been numerous attempts to identify the seed, the best known still remains that of Paul E. Beichner, CSC,[6] who saw in it a reference to the cardamom seed, used in both flavoring and medicine, and known as the "grain of Paradise." But in fact the grain remains finally mysterious, a clear and present sign of the entry of the supernatural into the narrative and a reminder of Mary, who brought it to earth. This entry of the supernatural apart, the strongest emotion the tale records is that of the boy's mother as she seeks him, and after his body is found – though then the abbot becomes involved as well. The tale belongs to a genre called "Miracles of Our Lady," which emphasized simple plots, overt sentiment, and the active intervention of Mary, often repaying devotion with a demonstration of her power, which was followed by the entry of her devout admirer into heaven. He may not have known it, but if he did, Chaucer rejected an alternative ending for the tale, one in which the Jews are converted. As the Prioress tells it, they are executed, every one who knew anything about the killing. In fact, the threat of hell is present in other of these "Miracles," and adds a half-hidden edge to their often senti-mental spirituality. Be sweet and innocent as a child or you'll burn forever in hell, they seem, as a group, to say, and as for those who are not part of our circle, well, we all know what will happen to them, don't we?

This mixture of religion and violence is not restricted to the *Prioress's Tale*. The *Man of Law's Tale* equally concerns the suffering of a religious innocent, and in it, too, violence, or the threat of violence, is never very far from the surface, a violence also informed deeply by racial complications and stereotypes.[7] The innocent in this case is a young Roman noblewoman named Constance, sent by her father to be the bride of a Muslim sultan who has promised conversion if they wed. Through many trials Constance proves worthy of her name, closely guarded by an ever-present divine power (since in an alien culture her nobility can not be counted upon to defend her) to protect her from the violence which surrounds her. The sultan's mother murders all the Christians at a welcome banquet for Constance, sparing only Constance herself, whom she sets adrift in a rudderless boat which finally takes her to northern England. There she falls in love with, and converts, a pagan king, King Alla, by whom she has a son, but Alla's mother equally turns against her, again setting her adrift, although this time, after further adventures, the friendly (and divinely directed) currents carry her to the ships of the Roman Emperor, who has just returned from taking revenge on Syria for her treatment there. Alla, in the meantime, has learned of his mother's deceit and killed her, and then gone to Rome to seek absolution for his crime. There he sees his son, recognizes a family resemblance, and is reunited. They return to Britain, where years later Alla dies; Constance then returns to Rome, where she is reunited with her father and friends, and spends her closing years in almsgiving and other works of mercy. The tale ends with a prayer that Christ will send all of us joy in heaven after the woe which we will find everywhere in the world.

Unlike the Prioress's Group, the *Man of Law's Tale* is concerned not with the entry of the supernatural into the characters' lives, even though God's immediate intervention is everywhere apparent. Indeed, in this tale divine intervention seems to operate almost mechanically, "according to the law," whenever Constance's protection requires it. The tale is less concerned with the realization of a personal spirituality than, as might be expected from one with the Man of Law's responsibilities, with the social implications of an ever-present God. The Man of Law himself remains one of the more enigmatic (or undeveloped) of the Canterbury pilgrims, traditionally interesting to Chaucerians because of his complex Introduction and Prologue, with their funny and ironic reference to Chaucer's tales, his soon-violated promise to speak in prose, and his extraordinary invocation to poverty, based on *De miseria condicionis humane*, a twelfth-century tract of Pope Innocent III which Chaucer has changed to make more affecting. Behind these stand, however, the hardly sentimental portrait of the *General Prologue*, in which, hard and punctilious, the Man of Law is represented as indeed speaking wisely, but only seeming to be judicious and dignified, and emerging finally as a well-dressed collector of fees who made his way by "writing," a word Chaucer uses almost as an indictment. His power, to paraphrase Mao, grows out of the barrel of a pen. It was specifically against such men that the not-yet-forgotten rising of 1381 was directed, and for all the sacred wonder which his tale manifests, there is also a note of exclusivity and power which attaches it easily to its teller, and forbids too any easy acceptance of the religious attitudes which it encodes, even when they attest to the powerful presence of the divine.

But like the *Prioress's Tale*, the Man of Law's combines violence and race in a way which suggests that, in some ways at least, religion for Chaucer encoded implicit social meaning, though often, too, it seems not untouched by a finally elitist sense of moral, ethical, and theological distinction. Thus, whether addressing Jewish religiousness in the *Prioress's Tale*, or Islamic in the *Man of Law's*, the tellers, and perhaps also Chaucer himself, seem frustrated by the realization that there are indeed roads which lead neither to Rome nor to Jerusalem. This sense of irreconcilability carries with it a threat not only to personal integrity, but also to a meeting of personal and social ends on which many of Chaucer's tales depend. The violence which each of these tales realizes – the execution of the Jews, the bloody defeat in battle of the Muslims – emerges from a sense of cultural unapproachability and a fear of difference which is embedded in a sense of the holy, and thus in forms which seem to define a pattern in human life.

It is true, of course, that other of the Canterbury tales are by no means innocent of violence, indeed violence is a continuing theme in many of them, redirecting lives, altering destinies. But the conjunction of violence, race, and religion is particularly powerful in these tales at least in part because it is directed at non-believers as non-believers, and it is not only the modern reader who feels the limitations which such assurance can bring. Not long after the Prioress has told her tale another of her group gives voice to his, and it begins with a pointed attack on the kind of religiousness which the Prioress has just exhibited.

The "Nun's Priest" does not actually belong to the Prioress, but he is hers in all but name. Chaucer does not allow many of his pilgrims a name, but from the offhanded way in which Harry Bailey greets him ("Come near, *thou* priest, sir John"), it seems clear that, thanks to the Prioress's elevated social class, priest or no, he is more or less under her thumb. But once he begins his tale it becomes equally apparent that, in reality, he is no such thing. The *General Prologue* had described the Prioress as elegant, even overly refined, or at least eager to seem so, one whose table manners were such that she carefully wiped her mouth so as not to leave a drop of grease in her cup; no morsel of food ever fell from her lips, nor did she dip her fingers deeply into the sauce. It's an odd way to describe a nun, and the fact that her table manners are described at all further diminishes her standing. Then, when the Nun's Priest comes to tell his tale, he begins with a description of a poor widow, living in a small cottage, leading a simple life of great economy – and we know at once what and whom he is getting at. The contrast could not be more obvious. In her dark little house she ate many a small meal, the Nun's Priest remarks. *She* at least had no need for fine sauces! Her diet was in accord with her "cote," but here Chaucer is making one of his many puns, since "cote" can mean both a small farm and also outer garment ("coat"). In other words, she acts according to the ideals implied by her station in life, unlike some other people I know!

The Prioress has been found elsewhere in the tale which follows, and John Broes, for example, identifies her with Pertolete,[8] the hen to whom the rooster in the tale is "married." But the tale which follows is one of Aesop's fables, one which, before the advent of Walt Disney and television, was known to many a child. As usually told, it recounts the story of the hen who warns her rooster-husband in a dream that he will be seized by a fox, but the vain and foolish rooster, who will not be warned by a mere woman, brushes her warnings aside, only to be caught by the fox soon thereafter. But the clever rooster then gets the fox to speak, and when he does so he opens his mouth, allowing the rooster to escape. He then rightly rejects the fox's feigned apology, acknowledges his own vanity, and insists that he will mend his ways. It is a tale which lent itself easily to medieval allegory, where the fox was one of the traditional symbols for the Devil, and where pride is seen as lying at the heart of many a human flaw.

Chaucer cleverly gives the tale another twist, for as the Nun's Priest tells it, it is the rooster, a loudmouth named Chauntecleer, who has the warning dream, and the hen, Pertelote, who laughs it off. Chauntecleer responds with a display of mock learning, but falls in with Pertelote's dismissal, if only to show that he is not a coward. It is also certainly a jab, as has been frequently pointed out, at the Monk and his long list of tragedies, of great men who fell from high standing, a kind of mock-heroic which treats Fate and Fortune in terms never anticipated by the earnest Monk, though it is not clear that Chaucer or his audience would have taken the contrast quite as solemnly as some criticism has. But the tale is deeply invested in antifeminism as well, and one of the reasons for this theme, as I have already noted, is riding not far away. The Nun's Priest makes his teaching really quite clear, warning that women's advice really isn't good, and citing the example of Eve tempting Adam to make his point. But no sooner is the example out of his mouth than he remembers that the demanding Prioress is not far off, and jokes nervously, "Pass over, for I said it in my game."

The reference to Adam is of course important, since what Chauntecleer learns is the lesson of all great ones, that of pride, a lesson which began with our first parents, Adam and Eve, who took the apple (a Latin pun: in Latin, the word for "apple" is *mallum*, the word for "evil," *mallus*) in the Garden of Eden, thus bringing all of humankind into sin. The supernatural which enters this tale, however, is less of God than of the Devil. Throughout, the tale's action follows not the narrative of Aesop, but that of the Book of Genesis, and the events which make it up – the temptation to pride by a demonic fox – are not accidental, but directed by the same God who saved Adam from the effects of *his* pride, and defeated Satan. This is an ironic but definitive way of recording the entry of the supernatural into human affairs, though the force which presents itself is destructive, not salvational. Emerging from a consideration of the ways in which we are all, whatever our rank, involved in Adam's sin, the entry of the supernatural is no less dramatic in the Nun's Priest's tale than in the Prioress's. Let all putative great ones recall that they came from Adam, the tale, very indirectly, insists, and are thus involved in his transgression, so sounding a theme which the 1381 rebels sounded too. But the tale encodes as well a description of the Prioress herself, who does not understand, according to the Nun's Priest, that her love of the court, good food, and elegant manners are distracting her from other, and more important, realities. Blinded by pride and the love of good living, she is following the fox. So take the fruit of my tale, the Nun's Priest insists at the end, and let go the chaff. Salvation is serious business, and as St. Paul reminds us, everything which is written can instruct us.

A great deal has been made of this tale, and there at least used to be a school of thought which insisted that it lay at the heart of the *Canterbury Tales* itself. But for all of its evident concern with morality, Adam and salvation, it is also about gender, though even here

Chaucer's thinking is not binary, and the constructions present in the tale are refracted through ways in which the Nun's Priest conceives of the larger teachings of Christianity. Pertelote is the cause of Chauntecleer's downfall; the Prioress is vain and fails to understand the extent of her own self-deception; the Bible teaches that Eve made a mess of things. It can not be said that these themes, or some version of them, are absent in Christianity, but as so often in Chaucer, other things are present as well. The Nun's Priest may indeed have uncovered the prideful pattern of human life (including his own), a pattern which he believes present in the Prioress and also, by extension, in her sentimental spirituality, but there is a third member of the group who has yet to be heard from.

It is interesting that two of the three women narrators in the *Canterbury Tales* are nuns who tell tales explicitly concerned with personal spirituality, and so with the entry of God into individual human lives, not only with the presence of God everywhere. In a way this distinction is not one which can be enforced absolutely – if God's presence is everywhere apparent, then the putative "entry" of God is really nothing more than the human perception of that presence, not its actual coming into being – but faith is sometimes actuated by encounter, whether miraculous (the *Prioress's Tale*), understood (the *Nun's Priest's Tale*), or a mixture of the two (the *Second Nun's Tale*).

After all, a direct engagement with religion constituted one of the few forms of authority open to medieval women. The priesthood, the episcopacy, the pontificate, even the study of most religious texts, were firmly in male hands. Few women, relatively speaking, could read Latin, and the universities, where the study of scripture and canon law were carried on, were closed to them. In spite of this now abhorrent discrimination, it is abundantly clear that, both during Chaucer's time and well before, many women were deeply invested in religious practices which they understood deeply, and which regulated and directed their lives and the lives of others who, for a great variety of reasons, responded either to them or to their teaching and example. Many of these, like the Prioress and the Second Nun, were members of religious orders, though others were not, and on the Continent (perhaps also in a few English cities like Norwich) groups of women known as "beguines" lived together, often under the protection of a local bishop, although not under religious vows. Still, they were dedicated to prayer, communal living, and performing good works in the larger community. In the late Middle Ages, roughly from the eleventh to the fifteenth century, a large number of religious books were written in or translated into the vernacular, so that those without Latin, both men and women, could read them.

These books disseminated knowledge of religious matters widely, and although there were some religious offices which were open to women there were constraints upon even that authority, whether educational, or in the person of, for example, a critical cleric who disapproved of women in general, and of learned or powerful ones in particular. But there were also both women and men who needed no intermediary. Mystics required no degree in canon law, and their teaching, at least when it was deemed both orthodox and inspired, carried its own authority. In the person of Catherine of Siena or Bridget of Sweden, mystics could and did influence princes and popes in spite of their gender, though often such women kept by them a male confessor who served, unlike the cleric who accompanies Chaucer's Prioress, as a kind of guarantee of both piety and orthodoxy.

But there were other devout women as well, who rejected an activist or social or political role in favor of a more private one. Some of these, particularly in England, became anchoresses, women who lived physically enclosed for life in a doorless room attached to a church whose masses they could both hear and see, and who could communicate with lay persons who brought them food and water, and with those who came to them for advice. We know, for example, that, in the early fifteenth century, the anchorite and mystic Julian of Norwich was visited by Margery Kempe, a deeply religious woman whose devout practices have long been the subject of study and controversy. Julian was not unlearned (the extent of her learning is still unclear, though there were friars in Norwich with whom she could discuss theology), but her authority, which was (and is) considerable, emerged from her religious experiences, and her reflections upon them, more than from anything else.

Medieval religious women did not love Christ as a way to power, but because they were religious persons. Yet their devout practices could indeed evoke authority, and so influence many about them. Depending upon person and circumstance, they could be the equal of any man, particularly in matters of religion, since their practices and beliefs were at the heart of a culture which both represented itself as being, and in some moments was, deeply religious. Chaucer himself had no hesitation about assigning to women much of the "work" of spirituality in his tales, and he seems to have done so because he estimated that there were aspects of religion which lay within the provenance of women, who often appeared to be the most faithful and frequent practitioners of a felt Christian faith. But he did not believe that the practice of Christianity was unproblematic, and, in the Second Nun's tale, represented, among other things, the difficulties involved in "being religious" at a time when much religious sentiment was largely conventional. In his portrayal of the Prioress's traveling companion, however, he reopened the matter of the Prioress's evident antisemitism through her Priest's complexly gendered reply.

Many of the concerns with race, gender, and class which now inform critical discourse in the humanities have deep roots, since, for centuries, authors have addressed or encoded them in their work, perhaps particularly in the conflicts they responded to or evoked. That is why it is neither surprising nor anachronistic to believe that they are at work in texts like the *Canterbury Tales*, where such conflicts flourish, and where their presence has long been understood. Thus when, following the Prioress, the Second Nun takes up her theme, she begins by saying that, in spiritual life as in secular, one must avoid the vice of laziness, and be both faithful and busy. Speaking in these terms, she seems to be holding up an ideal which was hardly attested to by her Prioress, since there is little in the Prioress's intellectual attitude which shows persistence, and more than a little which suggests prideful laziness. The Second Nun then goes on to offer a prayer to the Blessed Virgin, just as the Prioress had, and here the contrast between the two women becomes particularly clear. For where the Prioress had compared herself to a year-old child who is so innocent that she can hardly speak at all, the Second Nun calls Mary, among other titles, a "Well of Mercy" (the phrase was common in devotional literature of the period, and in his moving religious lyric "An ABC" Chaucer applies it to Mary, though usually it was applied to Christ), and as a sinful soul's cure. Like the Prioress, she asks Mary's help in telling her tale, remarking candidly, in what is an important theme in Chaucer, that faith is dead when it is unaccompanied by works. This is a perfect introduction to her tale, which tells the life of St. Cecilia in a way appropriate for her time, but which also reflects the Prioress's and the Nun's Priest's tales as well. In constructing her sacred fiction, a saint's life, the Second Nun sweeps the Prioress's sentimental racism aside, but challenges too the Nun's Priest's biblically based construction of gender, and the critique of women's spirituality which he had deftly implied. But she does so with a heart which is so evidently warm and devout that it is difficult to believe that either of the two persons with whom she is riding, both of whom, in one way or another, "outrank" her, will take offence at what she has to say. Hers is, like the Prioress's, a tale which is concerned with Christian spirituality and with the entry of the divine into human affairs, but is also in its way the most "feminist" tale in the Canterbury group.

In *Gender and Romance in Chaucer's Canterbury Tales,*[9] Susan Crane has pointed out that, in medieval romance, there are not many women "who successfully integrate masculine traits into femininity" (23), but that is exactly how, writing a saint's life, not a romance, Chaucer has represented Cecilia. For her, as for many women during her time and after, Christianity expanded the limits of gender, and that is how she tells her tale.

The tale, which Chaucer adapted from one or more sources, is at once simple and complex. As a saint's life it is almost as easily recognized now as in the medieval period, and recounts the way a woman known to history as Cecilia, a noble Roman woman of the third century, became a saint. Cecilia, who lived at the time of Christian persecution, preserved her virginity in the face of an arranged marriage with a Roman officer named Valerian, and then, with the assistance of Pope Urban I (d. *c.* AD 230) and a visionary old man whom we shall meet again in the next chapter, converted him to Christianity. Returning home after his conversion, Valerian is greeted by an angel, who carries two crowns of lilies (representing chastity) and roses (representing martyrdom), which he presents first to Cecilia, then to Valerian. Soon after, Tiburce, Valerian's brother, is converted, and not long after that both brothers are martyred for their new faith, having been encouraged by Cecilia in their last hours. Soon thereafter Cecilia herself is arrested. After a quick, able, and contentious argument with the judge who sentences her to death, she is led away to execution. But the executioner fails, with three strokes, to sever her head from her body, and the law forbids him any further strokes. Cecilia is thus able to preach for three days, converting many (though in pain all the while), before she in turn dies. The tale ends with a careful and curious reference to the church of St. Cecilia in which, "unto this day," Chaucer says, "men do service to Christ and to his saint."

As long ago as 1956 Mary Giffin published a little book called *Studies on Chaucer and his Audience*,[10] in which she pointed out that there was an intimate English connection to the church of St. Cecilia in Trastevere in Rome, since a new English Benedictine cardinal named Adam Easton had been appointed cardinal priest shortly after he was named cardinal, as was the custom for cardinals who were to live in Rome and so had no diocese of their own. But even more powerful than the evident association with Cardinal Easton was that with the reigning pontiff, Pope Urban VI, who reigned from 1378 until 1389, elected under threat from a Roman mob which, for reasons concerning financial advantage to their city, did not wish any but an Italian elected, and feared that any other pope would return the papacy to Avignon. Urban VI's election, together with the arrogant, unyielding face he turned on all opposition, precipitated what is still called the "Great Schism," a split in the medieval church which lasted from 1378 until 1417, and which effectively drove a wedge between Christians all across Europe, more than a century before the Reformation drove an even more lasting one. The English supported Urban VI against the new French antipope, Clement (he claimed the title Clement VII, and was in fact the Swiss son of a cousin of the French king), so that the attractive picture which the *Second Nun's Tale* paints of Pope Urban I, though completely unlike the aggressive, sometimes nasty personality which made Pope Urban VI so unpopular so quickly, may contain a hint of irony intended for those in the court who knew what Urban VI himself was really like.

But these historical associations, which would have been evident even if Chaucer did not write the tale to celebrate Adam Easton's elevation, faded into the background, but did not disappear, when he placed them into the mouth of the Second Nun. In its present position in the *Canterbury Tales*, it is no longer the appointment of an English cardinal or the workings of the schism which impress us, but the personality of St. Cecilia herself, dedicated to her faith and to her community, energetic, keenly aware both of the dangers she faces and the realities she has been called upon to represent. Her tale is a challenge to the sentimental racism of the Prioress and the easy contempt for women's spirituality which is present in the Nun's Priest's tale, but it is also a powerful statement about the beginnings of Christian spirituality, one which attests to the power and importance of faith in responding to divine intervention.

Most readers have been struck by Cecilia herself, powerful and perceptive, sensitive to her husband's demands upon her, but resolute in resisting them, and leading him into the ways of her Christian religion. In the early years of Chaucer criticism there was a misdirected argument which insisted that, since the Second Nun refers to herself as an "unworthy son of Eve" in her prologue, both it and tale must have been written for another pilgrim, probably a man! The reference to Eve should have indicated even to the unwary that the person referred to was more or less obviously a woman, but possibly what confused some of them was the powerful figure of Cecilia herself, even though her power is largely dedicated to the service of others. Indeed, one particularly important aspect of Cecilia's spirituality is her concern for her fellow-Christians, both in conversion and encouragement, particularly in her last days. This concern for the larger Christian community is a pervasive though sometimes circumscribed theme in Chaucer, who, often responding to what he found in his sources, generally represents a concern for others as integral to the practice of religion, and a censure to those, whether Pardoner or Prioress, who do not observe it.

But the entry of the supernatural, whether signaled by a grain, a fox, or a crown of flowers, has the effect of illuminating, rather than certifying, the significance of Christian faith, whether that of the boy in the *Prioress's Tale*, or of Cecilia and Valerian in the Second Nun's. But if the supernatural grain in the *Prioress's Tale*, and the demonic if symbolic fox in the *Nun's Priest's Tale* brought home to Chaucer's audience the ways in which the supernatural can touch human activity in ways and at times which are totally unexpected, the angelic apparition in the *Second Nun's Tale* registers a yet more powerful entry, one which broadens the significance of Cecilia's life and faith. The divine presence encoded in the crowns seems to promise active intervention in future human affairs, and so serves to strengthen the faith of Cecilia, Valerian, and all of Christ's followers.

There is also a way in which rightness can mislead, though Cecilia avoids the trap: when she challenges her bullying and powerful judge, she never forgets that it is Christ, not she herself, who is at the center of her religion, and part of her charge against him is that he has lost the respect of the people whose interests she, not he, finally serves. It is in this context that the *Second Nun's Tale* alludes to the Nun's Priest's representation of the exchange between fox and rooster with which his tale ends. Unlike the rooster who vies for intellectual superiority, Valerian defers to Cecilia, allowing divine grace an opportunity to assert itself. Even the admonitory conclusion of the *Nun's Priest Tale*, in which the rooster escapes from the fox's mouth by making him speak, gets a fresh twist in the Second Nun's tale. If the quick fox is one image of the Devil, then in his own way, this powerful and only apparently reasonable Roman judge is another, and while Chauntecleer leapt away from what seemed to be his doom, Cecilia embraces hers, offering an image and an example not only of quick wit, but of strong faith as well. The Nun's Priest's theology, with its harkening back to Adam and Eve, is set against the active evidence of divine grace which the Second Nun reveals and in which she rejoices.

But neither is the Second Nun uncritical of the Prioress, whom she both defends and reproaches. Although the non-Christians in her tale are Romans, not Jews, the unmistakable word which the Second Nun has for her lady Prioress is that it is a far, far better thing to endure persecution than to cause it. The falsity behind the merciless destruction of the Jews at the end of the *Prioress's Tale* is shown graphically at the end of the Second Nun's, in which Cecilia dies at the hands of her persecutors, thus showing her religion to moral, not physical, advantage.

I understand that there is a danger in all this of making the Second Nun sound too relevant, too much a spokeswoman for religion in our time, not hers. But this concern is only partly valid: though conscious of the fine interplay of gender and religion she may indeed be, her concern throughout is with faith, the entry of the divine (in the apparitions of angel and the mass conversions at the end) into human affairs, service to others, in particular to her fellow-Christians, and to the church, and these are hardly, *ipso facto*, modern preoccupations. Concerned with the power of the marginalized though she is, she does not neglect to recognize that of the state, or the necessity of forms. Her polished and articulate tale seems almost luminous compared with what has come before, though

Chaucer has clearly structured his collection of tales so as to insist that religion has many faces, the Pardoner's and the Summoner's among them, not hers alone. But the experience of reading the *Second Nun's Tale* is that of reading a confident, almost lyrical, hymn of praise, first of all for Cecilia, then for her husband Valerian and his brother Tiburce, and finally for Pope Urban I, all of whom follow the Christian faith which is at the heart of the tale. But the tale's spirituality reaches out to its audience, inviting them to admire Cecilia's courage and constancy, to wonder at her experiences, and then finally, as it lies within their power to do so, to share them.

6

Visions of Chaucer

About the time he began writing poetry, Chaucer developed an interest in a literary genre which scholars today call either "Dream Visions" or "Dream Narratives," from a literary convention in which the poet (or at least the narrative voice) is represented as recounting what has transpired in a dream, a practice which allows considerable latitude in the choice of theme, topic, and description.[1] The first chapter of this book set these early works into a biographical context, but it is good to remember how widespread the genre was, and how embedded in Chaucer's early art. Dream Visions were particularly popular in French poetry, and it was from French works like the thirteenth-century *Roman de la Rose* of Guillaume de Lorris and Jean de Meung that Chaucer came to understand the genre, though as with everything he did, he was never simply an imitator, and changed the conventions the genre upheld, more or less as it suited him.

The first of these "Dream Visions," the powerful *Book of the Duchess*, he wrote after the death of John of Gaunt's wife, Blanche, duchess of Lancaster, who died in 1368. Formal and mannered though it first appears, it is a searching, even psychological poem, in which the narrator-poet draws out a young grieving knight, who has lost his lady. The colors black (for the young grieving knight) and white ("Blanche," for the lady) inform an allusive and perplexing narrative, in which the narrator encourages the young knight to articulate, name, and so (perhaps) come to terms with what seems to be a very genuine grief. Grief is often formalized and made conventional in medieval poems, but in this one it is not difficult to believe that

24 Pilgrims around a Table (Hodnett No. 233)

Chaucer has indeed realized what John of Gaunt experienced after his young wife's death. It is an extraordinary poem, in which the visionary quality of narrative serves paradoxically to deepen the elegiac nature of the poem, and in which the literary and mythological allusions all but melt away before the young knight's pain and sorrow.

Five or ten years later (perhaps in the early 1380s; as I noted in the first chapter, it is difficult to be more precise), Chaucer began but failed to finish what was probably his second "Dream Vision," the *House of Fame* (also called the *Book of Fame*), which is as unlike the *Book of the Duchess* as it is possible for any poem to be. Although no one really knows why Chaucer began the poem, the narrative is boldly imaginative and daring, though the verse keeps to the short, four-stress couplets Chaucer had employed in the *Book of the Duchess*. This time, however, instead of the narrator meeting a young knight dressed in black in the forest, he is seized by an eagle, swept away in the bird's talons to meet a "man of great authority" – though we are never told who that man is, and just when he is about to appear (and so be named), Chaucer abandoned the poem. As it developed, the poem became more or less explicitly about the art of poetry, and in spite of its allusions to Virgil and Ovid, the eagle more or less obviously echoes Dante, so that his seizure of the narrator is a humorous representation of poetic rapture, of the poet being, as Ovid says, a *vates*, a holy seer, whose poetic vision is finally of divine origin. The echo of Dante is, however, ambiguous: it is in one way an English empirical representation of a continental literary convention, and a funny one at that, which shows that Chaucer's poetic rapture both is and is not like the one in Dante. The inspiration he claims is grounded less in an understood relationship between the political and the cosmic, than, for now at least, in an exploration of what other poets have seen before him – though those visions only anticipate what is to follow. The narrator of the *House of Fame* is more confused than godlike, and the powerful vision which is the poem seems to swirl about him, without his ever being very sure what it is going to mean. The image of the poet seized by an eagle is also a reminder that there are many kinds of poetic inspiration, and if Dante's is one, than Chaucer's, certainly, is another. Chaucer at once acknowledges Dante's influence and admires his genius, and at the same time pushes them away.

Chaucer's third great dream vision is the *Parliament of Fowls*, very probably connected to Richard II's marriage to Anne of Bohemia, as we saw in chapter 1, which mixes seriousness and humor throughout. An opening discussion of art and love gives way to the description of a highly problematic temple of love, and that in turn to the garden of Nature, in which, this being St. Valentine's Day, the birds are holding an animated conversation together, with just enough formality to constitute a parliament. In it, under the direction of Nature, the birds will choose their mates, beginning with three noble birds who are contending for the love of a formel (female eagle). Class, gender, art, and poetry are all at issue here, though so is humor, and when the almost comic courtly representations of the three great ones take too long, more lowly birds – the falcon, the cuckoo, the turtle-dove and the foolish goose – intervene with their ideas as to whom the formel should accept, but this resolves nothing, and Nature defers to the formel herself, suggesting, however, that she select the royal tercel (male eagle) as the noblest. The formel, however, asks for a year's delay to make her choice, and Nature agrees. The narrator then awakens.

It is possible to believe that Chaucer was now moving away from the genre of the dream vision, perhaps feeling confined by the conventions which made it up, gravitating, in any event, toward an art of narrative which he would shortly make his own. But he seems to have retained from the dream visions a sensitivity to the more plastic dimensions of narrative, a willingness to move easily from scene to scene, place to place, without being overly concerned about connections, and aware too that it was possible to realize in his texts other qualities than those present in empirical, cause-and-effect narrative. There is an aspect to Chaucer's art which sets it apart from even the greatest art of his age, a mixture of continental sophistication, English empiricism, and personal adventure, which is difficult to define, but easy to recognize. But it is not confined even by these great influences, and it is possible to believe that his early experiments, two successful, with dream visions, encouraged openings in his later narratives which finally would transform his art.

It is probably because of these later works that, in spite of these early visionary poems (and a fourth, the *Legend of Good Women*, which indeed begins as a dream vision but thereafter departs from the genre), Chaucer is not thought of as a visionary poet, nor is the *Canterbury Tales* usually reckoned to be a visionary work. But Chaucer began writing poetry fascinated with French Dream Visions, and with the artistic, intellectual and psychological freedom they brought. By the time he came to write the *Canterbury Tales* he had undertaken more formal narratives too, and *Troilus and Criseyde* in particular had nourished a more realistic (and ironic) narrative style, though one in which improvisation, juxtaposition, irony and humor play key roles. What also moved Chaucer was a narrative sense which both alluded to and often relied upon powerful visual effect.

Probably the opening of the *Knight's Tale* is one of the best-known examples. Returning to Athens with his new queen at his side, Theseus meets a company of ladies kneeling by the roadside where they know he will pass, all dressed in black and loudly lamenting their fate. Their fate is Theseus' too, and any knight's, and also that of every person: it is to die, and, for reasons which will become apparent in the next chapter, the *Knight's Tale* will indeed end in the death which the ladies' black lamentations foretell. But their sudden and dramatic appearance carries with it a moral imperative as well as a dramatic effect. For the ladies call Theseus to battle, to destroy the tyrant Creon, who has left the bodies of their husbands or sons to be eaten by dogs. Nor is it a detail that they are all members of the nobility: the social code indicates that, because they are nobles, they thus can claim Theseus as their champion, as one of them.

Strictly speaking, the appearance of the ladies is not a vision at all, any more than is any other unexpected turn of events, but its sharply defined visual component, its challenge to those who confront it, and its somewhat ambiguous character, share qualities which resonate in other tales, and which help to define a visionary thread which runs throughout the *Canterbury Tales*.

Chaucerian visions are rarely mystical, but they often have at least semi-religious resonances. They tend to be normative, not hegemonic, and almost invariably respond to a moral or even ethical dimension, though sometimes one with evident social implications. They also tend to be dichotomous, as in the opening scene of the *Knight's Tale*, juxtaposing a more or less explicit allusion to an apparently impersonal reality like Fate with a impending duty, in the case cited, somewhat exceptionally, the duty to make war. Curiously, the vision does not by itself confer authority, at least not in the manner of medieval mystics, whose visionary experience could move popes and kings, particularly when it suited them to do so.

The visions in the *Canterbury Tales* often concern themselves with the marginalized and the disadvantaged, with those who find themselves apart from the only apparently more rational and connected world of common discourse. In this respect, at least, they share certain qualities with Chaucer's understanding of religion, but with a few exceptions they appear in secular as well as in sacred contexts, and sometimes in very secular contexts indeed. Chaucer's visionary representations, both real and semi, are balanced between a sense of religiousness and narrative surprise, between the supernatural and the coincidental. They partake in qualities of each of these, but also have a discursive, narrative, and sometimes moral character, which seems informed as much by the poet's empiricism as by any impending revelation. But they reveal an aspect of Chaucer's art which is easy to overlook, and a sensitivity to them can prevent us from thinking about Chaucer as (and so reducing him to) a religious poet, a love poet, or even a narrative poet.

Compare, for example, the Wife of Bath's *Prologue* with the Wife of Bath's *Tale*. It is not right to call the *Prologue*, with its five husbands, social–sexual adventurism, and improbable successes, realistic, except perhaps when set against the *Tale*. It is usual to describe the tale as an Arthurian romance, albeit one which reflects its teller's personality or psychology. But everything about it bespeaks the path to a vision: the offense which leads to a quest, the quest which finishes with the discovery of an old woman who imparts what seems to be wisdom, the effect of that wisdom when the knight returns to the court from which he has been banished, and the final revelation of the even deeper wisdom which is implanted in subsequent events. Exceptionally, the "vision" here is words, not images, except perhaps in the imagined icon of an implied perfect marriage, and seems rooted in what F. Scott Fitzgerald called "the heart's ultimate need" – and the Wife of Bath's need, like Fitzgerald's, reflects the largely secular realities which make up her world. But the knight's experience is nothing if not transformative, and the serio-comic revelation he encounters certainly remakes his world. The intellectual playfulness of the tale is Chaucer's, and by trespassing on the estates of religion and theology, both of which were claimed by the universities and by those educated there, the tale all but demands the Clerk's rejoinder. It turns on coincidence – the knight's meeting with the old lady who gives him his answer – but it is a coincidence which has within it the seeds of the later Christian and moral judgment which the tale also embraces – but does not end with. All in all, it shows a young knight moving through the world of appearances, never entirely sure what is real and what is not, even at the end.

The *Clerk's Tale* is in its way a religious vision complete, and in some ways it also echoes the *Man of Law's Tale*. Juxtaposed to the *Wife of Bath's Tale*, it offers an alternative reality, even an alternative vision, specifically rejecting the Wife's coincidence, in favor of a more astringent attachment to law. Griselda's faithfulness, not so much to Walter as to God, is never finally allowed to be what the tale is "about." It is always "about" something other – or less – than God:

about Walter's meanness and madness, about fortitude, about the art of allegory itself, and its limitations when it comes to represent human experience. No wonder it ends with an exasperated acknowledgment of the Wife of Bath's genius! Religious it may be, but it also carries with it a sense of the importance of seeing. Walter's enclosed world is shattered by the requirements of those under him (but really those whom he serves, according to much medieval thought), and then later, by the realization of his wife's goodness; Griselda's is shattered by her understanding how her husband has changed, and then later by the larger world to which her steadfastness has given her access; even the readers' enclosed world is altered both by the realization that the tale functions at the level of allegory, but that allegory can neither account for nor excuse the Clerk's wild narrative.

Thus far I have been indicating that there is a visionary thread which runs through the *Canterbury Tales*, and one which forms an important dimension to Chaucer's art. It is not opposed to Chaucer's religiousness, but it is separate from it, and constitutes a way of seeing, of reorganizing apparently dichotomous realities like divine intervention and coincidence, changing the way we see events, not the events themselves.

Thus, when even as distinctly a religious tale as the *Second Nun's Tale* includes a vision, it is one which functions almost extraneously to the traditionally Christian orientation of the tale itself. Chaucer found this vision in his source, and does not elaborate upon it, so that its effect is to testify to the truthfulness of what follows, and perhaps to rescue it from sounding too conventional. In the course of the narrative, the Roman noblewoman and soon-to-be saint, Cecilia, tells her new husband, the Roman officer Valerian, that she must not make love with him, because she has an angel by her who will slay him if he seeks to consummate their marriage. Valerian, understandably, asks to meet said angel, and Cecilia sends him three miles out of town, along the Appian Way, to some poor people who will introduce him to "good Urban, the old." Valerian does as he is bid, and is soon introduced to Pope Urban, who praises Christ for having thus served his slave ("thy own thrall") Cecilia, and sent Valerian to him. At once there appears before both of them an old man clad in shining white garments, bearing a book written in letters of gold: "One Lord, one faith, one God, one Christendom, and

Father of all, above all, and over all, everywhere." The vision at first terrifies Valerian, who then comes to understand and believe what he has read in the book. The "old man" of the vision vanishes, and Pope Urban then baptizes him.

The previous chapter has already identified the religious dimension of this tale, but present too is the vision of an old man who appears before Valerian. As I noted, Chaucer found the apparition in his source, but that did not force him to include it, since he was adept at manipulating his sources, selecting what he wanted to keep, and letting go what he didn't. The old man is not an angel, since the angel which Cecilia promised Valerian will indeed appear before him when he returns to Rome, bearing two crowns, one with white lilies to symbolize Cecilia's and Valerian's chastity, the other with red roses to symbolize their martyrdom. At the meeting outside of Rome, however, the text focuses rather upon what can only be called the visionary quality of the apparition: the fact that the old man is dressed in shining white clothes, that his book is written in letters of gold, and that his appearance strikes terror into Valerian's heart. There is nothing coincidental about this most supernatural of visions, but it retains both the suddenness and the ambiguity, and also the moral imperative, which characterizes visionary apparitions elsewhere in the *Canterbury Tales*, even when they are at least apparently secular. Set in historical context, the words written in the book have particular importance, and the phrases "one faith, one God, one Christendom" almost certainly allude to the Great Schism which had placed one pope (Pope Urban VI, whom the English supported) in Rome, another (Antipope Clement VII, whom the French supported) in Avignon. But in the context of the *Canterbury Tales* it is the visionary character of the apparition which impresses, and the way it supplies strength to the weak and to Cecilia's cause, while motivating Valerian's conversion.

The character of an old man whose visionary implications propel the narrative appears elsewhere in the *Canterbury Tales*, and in one other place serves not only to advance the action, but to reformulate the terms under which the tale has begun. In the *Pardoner's Tale*, three revelers go out to search for Death, who has slain a friend of theirs and whom they mean to kill, when they also come upon an old man from whom they seek direction. Unlike the old man in the *Second Nun's Tale*, this one is not dressed in white nor carries a book written in gold. On the contrary, he is described as poor, and as completely wrapped up, except for his face, and he carries a staff instead of a book, with which he repeatedly strikes the earth, asking to be admitted, asking, in other words, to die. The three drunken young men are rude to him (it's not personal, they are rude to everyone), but he nonetheless explains that he must find "a man" who will exchange his youth for his great age, and failing that, he must remain alive for as long as God wills. He thus is able to tell them where to go to find death, so returning the young men to their quest, which will indeed end in the death they had sought.

Various attempts have been made to explain the old man, whether as the Wandering Jew or as a messenger or a personification of Death, or simply as an old man, though in similar tales the person who offers direction is a hermit or a philosopher, or even Christ himself. Here, however, he is none of these things, and his role is not only to offer direction, but also to sound the desperation of the quest on which the young men are bent, and to set it against an echo of the fantastic, but one which does not partake in the supernatural. Unlike the old man who appears before Valerian, and who manifests, in his dress and in his appurtenances, evidence of his divine origins, this one is simply uncanny. He has indeed visionary qualities, though these appear only to Chaucer's audience, not to his, and his unexpected intervention, together with the morality he holds out to the young men – quoting "holy writ," he remonstrates with them about their manners – serve to identify him with one of those visionary moments into which Chaucer permits the normative realism in which he delights to slip, so allowing into the narrative a quick, even a passionate realization of the world beyond the actual, a vision of another way of seeing.

Yet if the *Canterbury Tales* includes within it visionary utterances, it also includes their opposite, tales which stand against any visionary, indeed any supernatural representations, and which, whether explicitly or implicitly, defy the philosophical acceptance of supernatural revelation upon which many of the other tales depend. Tales like those told by the Pardoner, the Canon's Yeoman, the Manciple, and the Physician pay a kind of superficial tribute to a sense of the supernatural which at heart they and their tellers or their protagonists secretly, though not always consciously, despise. Thus the Pardoner's self-serving representation of a debased morality gives the sense of approving the very philosophy the Pardoner himself only apparently rejects. The Canon's Yeoman's attack on uncritical credulity hardly supports the religious faith to which it finally appeals. The Manciple's disapproving approval of self-interest flirts with, but then rejects, any more noble motivation. And the Physician's appeals to Nature hardly disguise the hard-headed impersonality of his thinking. There is a streak of what I can only call proto-modernism in these tales which stands against their sentiments, some of them religious, and which runs deep. I have discussed this aspect of the *Physician's Tale* elsewhere,[2] but it is not present only there, and the final tales of the Canterbury group display a concern for the power of religion and that of modernity.

It may seem hard to call these tales, collectively or individually, anti-visionary, particularly since I have identified and discussed a visionary moment at the very heart of the *Pardoner's Tale*. But in their studied avoidance of the philosophical implications of so many of the tales, and in the symbolic resonances present in the pilgrimage on which they are engaged, they entail a kind of collective turning away from the possibility of symbolic meaning to a world of hardened surfaces, in which motivation is based on self-interest, and faith in anything unseen is simply a sign of naiveté. It is not an altogether attractive world these tales describe, but neither is it unfamiliar. Changes having been made, it is startlingly modern.

All great literature is in some sense visionary, and the *Canterbury Tales* is no exception. But apart from the familiar connotations of the word there is something else, an echo throughout of a world which lies behind the present one, but which cannot be described in conventionally religious language. At moments throughout the text, both in religious tales like the Second Nun's and in less religious tales like the Pardoner's, Chaucer introduces, usually from his sources, a visionary moment, which serves at once to surprise character or audience, and to direct attention, often to a morally ambiguous reality, which deeply informs the text.

These are not the visions of mystics – unsurprisingly, since Chaucer was no mystic – but they are integral to his art and to his way of seeing. Whether individually or together, they do not establish power, which is located elsewhere, in religion, in the work of individuals, and in the state, but they do lay claim to authority, even though the authority they call upon is often that of the apparently marginalized. In the end, the visions of the *Canterbury Tales* indicate, however fleetingly, values which direct belief, and so inform action. In this sense at least, the *Canterbury Tales* is a visionary work.

7

Death

Although we do not know the day in October 1400 when Geoffrey Chaucer died, there is reason to believe that he had considered the eventuality for some time. Recently he had moved to a tenement (since torn down) in the garden of the Lady Chapel of Westminster Abbey. It was this move which would lead to his being buried in the Abbey after his death, thus eventually beginning, after his grave had been moved to a new tomb in 1556, the now famous "Poets' Corner," and so starting the process which led, for better or worse, to the present canonizing of his work. But it is hard to believe that, even when he was contemplating his own death, Chaucer's thoughts often turned to the general apocalypse which some of his contemporaries were expecting, though he had a skeptical turn of mind, and in practice seems to have dismissed few things unheard. Still, there is no real indication that he believed that the world was dying too, and when his thoughts about death do register in the *Canterbury Tales* it is with the sense that life will carry on, that death is one event among many, and that, whatever else may happen, the world as we know it is unlikely to perish any time soon.

Christopher Daniell's *Death and Burial in Medieval England*,[1] which combines historical and archaeological evidence with literary, shows the pervasiveness of the topic, and the multitude of ways in which medieval persons addressed it. What stands out, both in Daniell and in Chaucer, is the public role death assumed, the almost easy place it held in everyday discourse.

This is not an unusual state of affairs in late medieval England, where even criminals were often buried facing east, in expectation

Troilus and Cresyde (Hodnett No. 1009)

of a final resurrection, and yet where the facts of bodily decomposition were so widely understood that late medieval English coffins often have drainage holes to hasten the process, and the movement from one grave to another of decomposed, or largely decomposed bodies, was a relatively common practice. Corpses were more in evidence as well, even though methods of embalming were, by modern standards, still somewhat primitive. The picturesque covered gate which leads into many a country churchyard was called the "lich gate," the body gate, since it was customary to leave the body there while most of the mass for the recently departed was being said or sung. The gate had a roof to protect the body from rain, but, in an age before modern undertakers, it often smelled so strongly that it could be brought into the church only briefly, for a final blessing and prayers. Within the church there were not only the entombed bodies of the eminent dead, but sometimes chantries too, decorated chapels usually established by a legacy, in which, as we have seen, daily mass was said for the soul of the benefactor, and, depending upon the terms of the agreement, for those of his family members also. Chaucer's Parson won't touch them, but there were those who would.

Decomposed and decomposing bodies also figure prominently in the literature and the art of the period, and appear both in handbooks instructing the reader on the "art of dying," on how to die well, and in numerous poems of the period. Carved effigies on the tombs of the great figure prominently in many medieval churches. Yet in spite of the many evidences for death that were present to everyone, it is difficult to know how far a putative fear of death, the *timor mortis conturbat me*, actually gripped the population as a whole, except during periods of plague or civil war. Still, some English country churches to this day display late medieval wall paintings of St. Christopher, a popular saint whose image, in silver, the Yeoman wears upon his chest, and whose duty it was, among other things, to protect from injury and sudden death. Some believed that they would live through any day in which they looked upon his image, in a church or elsewhere. The desire was not unreasonable. Daniell points out that the recent excavation of a medieval graveyard at Taunton showed that no women buried there had lived beyond age 45, and that the "most likely age to die" (133) was between 25 and 30, and then 30–35, but that those who reached 50 "were likely to live much longer" (134). Life expectancy dipped during the Black Death to 17.3 years "for men born between 1348 and 1375," Daniell notes (133), rising to 32.8 years in the fifteenth century. Such figures change dramatically from place to place, but can give some indication of what was involved, and what was expected, in the important matter of human mortality.

It is thus not surprising that, as soon as we escape from the idealized realism of the *General Prologue*, we encounter death, sudden, undeserved, and with dramatic social implications. I have said in an earlier chapter that the *Knight's Tale* is deeply concerned with love, and so it is, but it is also concerned with death, indeed love and death seem often to run together in Chaucer's mind, as in so much Western literature generally. When we look at the tale as a whole, the links appear clearly. It is opened by Theseus, a hero from antiquity, but since in Chaucer's day Athens was ruled by a duke, he appears here very appropriately as the Duke of Athens. In an opening scene which is at once visionary and political, Theseus is returning home from a conquest of the Amazons, together with his new Amazon queen, Hippolita, her beautiful young daughter, Emily, and a great company of knights. But suddenly that visionary company of ladies dressed in black appears before him, kneeling beside the highway, more or less obviously waiting for him to come by. It is indeed a vision, and one rooted in love, but it is also an omen of what is to come.

Their plight, expressed in their dress and behavior as much as by what they say, causes Theseus to stop in his tracks, and agree to attack with his army Creon, King of Thebes, who has tyrannically killed the men who were these women's lovers, husbands, and sons, and who has left their unburied bodies to be eaten by dogs. But Theseus signals not only his compassion but more importantly (for Chaucer) his nobility, and he does so from the moment the women appear before him. He leaps down from his charger, his heart moved by "pity," a quality in Chaucer which involves a complex recognition of what it means to be human, but one which he generally associates with nobles. After the battle Theseus has agreed to fight on their behalf, there are found, in a pile of bodies, two knights, neither fully alive nor fully dead, both of royal blood. Theseus has them sent to Athens to be kept in prison until death, since, though it would be unknightly simply to kill them outright (this is fiction, after all), it also would be dangerous to his state to allow them to go free. As V. A. Kolve has pointed out in *Chaucer and the Imagery of Narrative*,[2] in some ways prison is one of the controlling images of the tale, indeed in some ways the young knights never leave it, but are imprisoned by a love which borders on obsession, so that their love becomes a form of bondage, and gods, whether psychological, real, or planetary, impede human freedom as finally as any wall.

The two young knights of royal blood, Palamon and Arcite, are entombed beside a garden into which comes, one fine day in May, beautiful, yellow-haired young Emily, who is gathering red and white flowers, and singing like an angel. Once they have recovered from their nearly mortal wounds, they see her and are smitten. The *Knight's Tale* has begun.

Here as elsewhere, Chaucer manifests a very strong visual sense, and individual scenes, as well as individual characters, often impress themselves. The black dresses which the ladies wear point vividly not only to the many deaths which have moved them to action, but also to the sense that death is a part of life, intruding upon our moments of triumph, reminding us how short human life really is. "I tell you, we must die," they seem to be saying. Theseus, though a man of action, gets the message, and springs to the defense, almost as though it is Death itself he is going to oppose, not simply a tyrant.

But the young knights, being young, don't understand. Chaucer insists that they don't, both by the naive and bitter argument they have over which of them really loves Emily (though they are both prisoners and she hardly knows that they're alive), and also by the formal symbolism present in the red and white flowers which Emily picks as she sings her May-day song. The garden through which she moves has echoes not only of Paradise, and so of the innocence which first attached to Adam and Eve, but also of the ironic and contested garden in the *Merchant's Tale*, where blindness and innocence, foolishness and insight, also play a part. But the garden in the *Knight's Tale* seems, if momentarily, transfigured. If, in a way familiar to readers of literature, its white represents (among many things) innocence, purity, and newness, its red stands for the opposite: blood, love, experience of life and the world. The many connotations of red are as clear to us as they were to Chaucer's audience, and though not all brides still dress in white, or cowboys ride white horses, the connotations of white on which Chaucer relied, changes having been made, are ours as well as his.

The two knights continue their love-contest over Emily, and when Arcite is released (it turns out that he has connections) he is forbidden to return to Athens upon pain of death. He proves his love for Emily by returning anyway, and in the disguise of a "page of the chamber," an office Chaucer will not have forgotten from his own youth, whose duties include chopping wood and carrying water, not the sort of work expected of a knight, except he be in love. Palamon meanwhile is left to die in prison, even though when Arcite is released he tells him that Emily is so close by that his prison has become a Paradise. But he doesn't think so, and escapes.

Now comes a scene which medieval readers would have understood at once, but which modern readers sometimes laugh at. After he has escaped into the countryside, Palamon hides in a bush when he hears someone, who turns out to be Arcite, roaming happily through the forest, singing away, but then suddenly falling into a funk, when he thinks how far he is actually from attaining Emily's love. Conventionally, he is up and down like a bucket in a well, Chaucer says, or like a Friday (which some in the fourteenth century believed to be an unlucky day, probably because it was the day of Christ's death), which now shines brightly, now pours with rain. But when Palamon hears him complain (he does so out loud), he leaps out of his bush and declares his hatred of him, and his love of Emily. They agree to fight to the death, and Arcite promises to return the next day with arms enough for both of them, so that they can do so. As if all that was not enough, the next day, while they are fighting, Theseus and his court, out for a hunt in the forest, come upon them. Palamon and Arcite are fighting so fiercely that they are blind to the group's approach, and until Theseus again leaps off his steed and, with his sword drawn, parts them, they will not stop. At once Palamon admits who they are, and confesses their mutual love for Emily. Typically, Theseus is more struck by the admission of guilt than by the confession of love, and, sounding again the theme of death, cries "You shall be dead, by mighty Mars the red!," giving the color red yet another meaning. And but for the women, they might be. At once the Queen, Emily, and all the ladies in the company realize that love, not lawbreaking, is the cause of these difficulties, and so they burst into tears, crying, in a line which recalls the first meeting with the Theban women by the highway, "Have mercy, Lord, upon us women all!" Again, Theseus takes the point and relents, offering, instead of an executioner, a tournament to take place in a year's time, which will decide which of the two shall have Emily's hand in marriage, and more besides, though he does not know it at the time.

At this point almost every reader becomes aware that he or she is firmly in the jaws of fiction. For one thing, women don't behave that way, except in fictions, as the Wife of Bath might say, written by men. For another, everything that happens *is* a little too convenient: Palamon perfectly positioned in a bush so that he can hear Arcite complain about his lot in life, Theseus and the court coming along at just the right moment. What's going on? "Fate," might have been the answer of some, at least, in Chaucer's audience. "Either that or Providence." Chaucer doesn't simply raise these questions implicitly, however: he brings them home with a vengeance. When the tournament takes place, Arcite wins, but, as we have seen, is killed afterwards in what looks like a freak accident. Death strikes again, limiting human ambition and glory, in an apparently impersonal (but narratively convenient) way. His horse throws him, and he breaks his sternum on the saddle pommel: that means he will certainly die, but not immediately, and so will have time for some last words. So the freak accident isn't a freak accident at all. All this time the actions of the characters have been watched over by the gods: especially by "mighty Mars the red" to whom not only Theseus but also Arcite pray, and also by Venus, who favors Palamon. What looked to humans like an accident was actually an event directed by the gods, in which a Fury, here a divine being who acted as a source of retribution from the underworld in the service of the gods, was sent by Pluto at the request of Saturn (whom Venus had importuned), to frighten Arcite's horse so that he threw, and thus killed, poor Arcite.

But Chaucer really didn't finally believe that Fate, whether directed by the gods or not, ruled our lives.[3] He was a student, as we have seen, of the Roman philosopher and civil servant Anicius Manlius Severinus Boethius (c.480-c.524), to whom he may have felt a personal and philosophical attraction, since they were both public men, who mixed in their daily lives with the very great, but who also enjoyed an intellectual life, as well. Chaucer doesn't state his response to the questions he raises bluntly, but he does, wittily, allude to Boethius, if only so that those who share his interests will see where he is going. For example, the questions which we have seen Arcite pose when dying are those which also moved Boethius, as he was in prison, having fallen from a high position and awaiting execution. In the end he was executed, garrotted in prison in AD 524 at the express order of the Arian Gothic King Theodoric, for the high crime of having corresponded with Constantinople. During the very difficult period between his arrest and execution he wrote *The Consolation of Philosophy*, a book well known to Chaucer, who probably shared the general belief that Boethius was a Christian (the issue is still not settled, though probably he was), and had in fact translated, from Latin into English, part of the little treatise in which Boethius, considering his own death, sets the workings of providence above those of fate.

The difference is that Boethius poses answers, or at least philosophically considered responses, to the questions he raises, and does so in the face of execution. Arcite does not, but that need not mean that he didn't understand his plight, or that, in the face of death, he gave way to despair, even if, as far as Chaucer lets us know, he can never, like Troilus, finally laugh at his plight. In spite of Boethius, Chaucer represents Arcite, like Theseus, as firmly rooted in the world he knows, even when death sweeps away everything he has been expecting. At the end he simply rejects the philosophical reassurances which Boethius articulates, and insists on facing, with courage and finally with sensitivity, what is to come. From this perspective it can be said that Arcite, and perhaps also Chaucer's own perspective, is *not* that of Boethius, though they respond to it, while remaining attached to the reflective but passionate conjunction of love and death which runs throughout the tale. But even when the highly personal actions of the "gods" have been taken into account, there is also an utterly impersonal aspect of death, one which humans can only name, never finally explain.

Thus, in the midst of a long romance, Chaucer poses serious questions. Does life have intrinsic meaning, or only what we impose upon it? If human love is a part of nature, why is it so disruptive of human constructions? Does death restore order, or is order simply something we name that gives a kind of balance to our lives? And in the long run, do our actions matter, or not?

Quite apart from the philosophical importance of these questions, they also function artistically. Throughout, Chaucer has almost gone out of his way to make the *Canterbury Tales* seem more disconnected, more random, than it in fact is, though he avoids making such order as there is at all obvious, or locating it in one place, for example in religious consolation. One pilgrim (the Miller) jumps in and insists on telling his tale even when the Host wants the Monk to proceed him; another pilgrim (the Friar) stops the Wife of Bath after her Prologue, precipitating an exchange with yet a third pilgrim (the Summoner), which will lead to an apparently unexpected exchange; just as the pilgrimage is nearing Canterbury, and it seems reasonable to expect that things are drawing to an end, they are approached by two men whom they have never seen before, but when one proves talkative (the Canon's Yeoman) the other, the Canon, gallops away again. And yet in each case, and in others as well, the effect of these apparent interruptions is to cast what has just been said, or what is about to be said, against a larger frame of reference. In 1967 Robert M. Jordan published *Chaucer and the Shape of Creation*,[4] a study which, among other things, showed that in some important ways Chaucer was deeply informed by Gothic art, and that his own art was architectonic, so that contrasts between the small and the great, the immediate and the general appear throughout his fictions. In the same way both the interruptions I have mentioned, and the questions Arcite poses as he is dying, reflect the larger issues which run through the *Canterbury Tales* as a whole, and remind the reader to look beyond the appearance of randomness and meaninglessness to the larger possibilities which lie beyond them.

But it is a mark of Chaucer's essential integrity that he does not minimize the effects of disorder in the world he creates, and that many of his characters, like Arcite, do not achieve a full understanding of the limitless backdrop against which their individual actions are cast. His true heroes are less characters like the Knight, the Squire, and the Physician's Virginius, than those like the Parson, the Yeoman, and the Man of Law's Constance, who through endurance and duty come to understand the purpose of the universe and their place in it. But it is not an understanding which is easily won, and Chaucer displays considerable sympathy for those like the Miller and the Friar, the Prioress and the Pardoner, whose understanding is characterized by ignorance, willfulness, and self-centeredness and who cannot therefore see so far. These characters are represented as living in a world where random chance prevails, where events seem

disconnected to causes, and where grace and gesture become ultimate human attributes. Dying Arcite, no Boethian, shows the
strengths and weaknesses of most of us. "What is this world?" he
asks. "What can we ask to have? Now with our love, now in our
cold grave, alone, without any company!" But in a moment of ex-
quisite sensitivity and generosity quite beyond the very few indications we have had of his character, he turns to Emily and, setting
aside the strife and rancor which have so long been between them,
meekly suggests to Emily that if ever she would be a wife, she would
do very well to "forget not Palamon, than gentle man." Then he
dies.

But there's more to Emily than either of the once-young knights
thought, and more to this scene than the realization of human love
we explored in an earlier chapter. From one point of view, after all,
the knights had conceived of Emily more or less as an object to be
contended for, in the way superficial modern readers think "every-
body in the Middle Ages" thought of women. But she has her god
too – the goddess Diana, who had appeared to her the night before
the tournament, when she went to pray for deliverance. What *she*
wants, half-Amazon that she is, is to be delivered from both Palamon
and Arcite. "I am," she reminds Diana, "of thy company, a maid
who loves hunting, and to be in the wild woods – and not to be a
wife and be with child." No wonder she was with Theseus and
Hippolita when they found the knights fighting in the forest. Hunting is her thing; making love is not.

But when Diana appears – the scene is described very dramatically, as a divine apparition should be – she tells the young woman
to forget it, that she must be married. The gods have decided that
she must, and to one of the two young men in question, though
which one she is not at liberty to say. Her intervention is the first of
many in which a woman's aspirations are thwarted by impending
male authority, but what matters too is that the goddess to whom
Emily has been praying is not only the goddess of the hunt, an activity which ever ends in death. She is also the goddess of childbirth,
an aspect Chaucer emphasizes when describing Diana's statue as
having a woman giving birth before it. The woman even calls out to
Diana (who in this aspect of her divine being is called "Lucina"),
"Help! For you may best of all!"

Chaucer's young knights are young no longer. Like all of us, they have enjoyed (even in prison, but especially outside it) the privileges of youth, but now it is time to pay the piper, and the piper is Age and Death. "This world is but a thoroughfare of sorrow," Theseus' old father, Egeus, tells him. "And we are pilgrims, passing to and fro. Death is the end of all our earthly woe." But Theseus will have none of it. After everything that has happened – the destruction of hope, the end of love, of life itself – he closes this remarkable tale with his "First Mover" speech, which also derives from Chaucer's reading of Boethius. In it, he alludes to the "First Mover," who is usually understood as the Christian God, but as a pagan Theseus' language modifies Boethian ideas, and is not specifically Christian. The concept of the "unmoved mover" had been developed in 1259 by St. Thomas Aquinas, for whom it was a proof, in the *Summa contra gentiles* (I, 13), for God's existence, important because Aquinas thought it could lead to knowledge of God even in those, like Theseus, who lack Christian revelation. For Theseus, however, this First Mover, has placed limits on all things; it alone is perfect and stable. So it is wisdom, Theseus says, to make a virtue of necessity, and accept what we can't change: fate in life, death at the end of it. For all of the disorder which he has witnessed throughout his life, Theseus, like most of us, is rooted philosophically in this world, not the next.

The *Knight's Tale* conceives of death in the highest possible terms, philosophical and moral, implicitly acknowledging its unpredictability, and testifying to its power as well. Death may be a part of life, even an accomplishment of it, but it still comes suddenly and unannounced, to the young, as it does at the beginning and the end of the narrative. The tale has to do with other things too, with heroism and honor, with war and governance, all of them human constructions and great in their way. But as Egeus says, death is the end of all our earthly woe.

There is no shortage of death in other of the *Canterbury Tales* as well, from the *Nun's Priest Tale*, which briefly sounds the theme of murder, to the *Clerk's Tale*, in which, however, the deaths turn out to be invented, though intended to remind the reader of those which are not. But one other tale where death is as real as it comes is the *Pardoner's Tale*, one of the strangest tales in the Canterbury group, and in its own twisted way, one of the best. It is told by a Pardoner, a functionary whose duties have now been assigned to the trash can of history, but he filled an important function in his day. His job, as we have seen, was to supply pardons to people who had already been to confession, since according to medieval penitential theory there was still some punishment left in the next life for the penitent, though by the simple act of offering money for purposes sanctioned by the church, even this punishment could be avoided. As I have already noted, in the Middle Ages many functions which are now addressed by state and local government were the responsibility of the church – and there was only one church going. Pardoners then would ride about the countryside, with the bishop's permission to preach in church and so "win silver" as Chaucer puts it in the *General Prologue*. He is careful to emphasize the word "win."

This is the man who sings to us of death. There is a long prologue to his tale in which he warns the other pilgrims how he operates. After brandishing his credentials, he tells the pilgrims, he begins with a few words of Latin to intimidate the ignorant country people, and then produces his phony relics to help cure their livestock, and improve their lives and properties generally. Only cuckolds, he says, and any who have committed a "horrible sin," cannot be helped by what he has to offer, and had better stay away. Then he tells his tale.

Like the *Knight's Tale*, this one begins with the report of death, though from the start the Pardoner announces his theme, "Cupidity is the root of all evil." Cupidity means more than the love of money, though it means that too. It is a disposition of mind and heart which places earthly things above spiritual, the apparently real before the truly real. Beginning with a deformity can only produce a deformity, the Pardoner teaches, though he himself is a good example of exactly what he is preaching about. In Flanders, the Pardoner begins, there were three young thugs, guilty of all the sins imaginable, and nasty to boot. But now suddenly the Pardoner interrupts his tale, and preaches against drunkenness, gluttony, gambling, and swearing. Among many examples, he insists that Eve ate the forbidden apple because of Gluttony, one of what were called the "Seven Deadly Sins," actions and dispositions to act which were not regarded as sins in themselves, but as dispositions which incline one towards sin. He rants on, but then remembers his story, and returns to it. Early one morning, he continues, as these young thugs sat drinking in a tavern, they saw a body being carried to the grave. "Go quick," one calls to a servant boy, "and find out who that is. And mind you get the name right." But the boy knows who it is: it was the nasty thug's old friend, who was slain only the night before when, sitting drunk on a bench, a stealthy thief called Death, who kills all the people hereabouts, came quietly along and took his life.

There is nothing accomplished in this death, Chaucer seems to say, and even though the thug in question is no victim of Creon, the three young thugs, like Theseus before them, set out to deal with death. Their mission both is and is not a joke, as they rush out in search of Death, whom they expect to kill. Before long they meet with the semi-visionary Old Man whom we have already encountered and who is likewise seeking Death, not to kill him, but so that Death will take *his* life – for he must live until he can find someone who will exchange his youth for his great age. Not even Death can take him, he tells the three young thugs, until he does. They demand of him to know where Death is, and he tells them: "See that oak? You'll find him right behind it." But when they run to the tree what they find is eight bushels of gold coins – a number divisible by two but not by three – instead. Foolishly delighted with their find, they forget their quest, and send the youngest of them off to town for some food and drink with which to celebrate. But when he returns they kill him, so as to get his share. They then fall upon the drink he brought back, and die almost at once: the young man had the same thought, and the drink was poisoned.

If the *Knight's Tale* showed death in life, the *Pardoner's Tale* shows life all but saturated with death, not so much to prove that there is life in death (though that is part of the Pardoner's con), as to prove it inescapable; it will get you in the end, do what you may. But what sets the *Pardoner's Tale* apart more than anything is its strange Buddhist source. Surprising as it sounds, the work we now call the *Pardoner's Tale* began life around the third century somewhere in Asia, as a *Jātaka*, one of a collection of about 500 very short narratives told by Buddhist monks.[5] These tales were very popular, and certain of them became detached from the collection and made their way West, usually through Arabic and other intermediary versions. The original story concerned a young Buddhist monk who, with his Brahmin master, was captured by a gang of 500 thieves and sent for ransom while his master was held captive. But left in this uncomfortable position, the master ignored the word of warning he had from the young Buddha, and recited a charm which brought down a shower of gold upon his captors, thus obtaining his release. At once the first gang of robbers was approached by a second, also 500 strong, who demanded the gold. The first band refused, but pointed out the Brahmin: but he could not repeat the trick before a year had passed, too long for the impatient robbers, who killed him, and then attacked and killed the first band too. But then the second band fell out among themselves, and fought until only two were left. One of these stood guard over the gold, while the other went for food. When the food came it was poisoned, though the second robber killed the first before tasting it. At last the young monk returned with his now superfluous ransom, and saw at once what had happened. "My master in his self-will has destroyed not only himself, but a thousand others, too. Truly, they who reap gain by misguided and mistaken means shall reap ruin, as did my master."

The Buddhist attitude toward death is of course very different from the one which emerges in Chaucer's tale. The robbers are not held "to blame" for the catastrophe they brought about, partly because they are robbers, partly because Buddhism does not attach blame to individuals quite as easily as Christianity. Take the professed theme which the Pardoner brings to his work, *radix malorum est cupiditas* – cupidity, or perhaps desire, is the root of all evil. If by desire you mean cupidity, the love, say, of money, no problem. And if you wish to add that it is the root of all evil, all well and good. But if, in a more Buddhist turn of mind, by desire you simply mean desire, and if you add that it is the root of, well, everything, then there will be those for whom you are no longer preaching Christian doctrine. St. Augustine, for one, insists that we define ourselves by what we love, an action which involves an individual will which in turn is predicated on an idea that there is a self. We approach God *non ambulando, sed amando* – not by walking but by loving – in his famous turn of phrase. And loving requires a loving individual, as well as one who is loved.

The same goes for the two tales I have just told. Chaucer's version, which had no doubt already traveled a long way, both physically and philosophically, from its Buddhist source when he encountered it, is unmistakably Western and Christian. There is blame (though surprisingly little guilt) in good measure, and it is loaded firmly onto the shoulders of the three young thugs, who imperil their souls not only by being willing to murder, but by drinking, swearing, even eating too much, almost as if these things were the thin edge of the wedge. It is certainly the case that the audience is meant to take a sort of pleasure in their multiple deaths, indeed, we can almost hear the congregation murmur "quite right too," and reach for their wallets, as the tale comes to an end. The Buddhist version, on the other hand is a good deal more compassionate, even though it is also a good deal more bloody. Humans err, but are not as a consequence damned forever, and even robbers, who in the *Jātakas* have a somewhat ambiguous reputation, must be regarded with a certain guarded respect. They certainly earn no merit by their actions, but neither does the pretentious and self-willed master, who is held to be the cause of the catastrophe, seeking his advantage, like the robbers, by mistaken and misguided means. The reduced numbers of those involved in Chaucer's version have the effect of focusing the narrative dramatically, and making the fact of death even more telling. Death is no longer a part of life, even when unexpected, but the result of sin: you die both because you commit sin and because Adam did, and if you die unabsolved you may expect the worst hereafter. Thank goodness for penance and forgiveness, or so says the corrupt Pardoner, who by his person calls into question his own argument.

At the very end of the *Pardoner's Tale* a scene takes place which sets a sort of coda on the tale. The Pardoner seems suddenly to have forgotten what he has been saying, and the way he has revealed himself, and turns to Harry Bailey, the most down-to-earth person on the pilgrimage, and tries to sell him a phony relic. "Be the first," he tells the hardheaded innkeeper, "since you are the most enveloped in sin. Kiss all the relics. Get your wallet out at once." Wrong man, wrong approach. "No, no," Harry Bailey replies. "You would make me kiss your drawers, and swear it was the relic of a saint, even though it was stained with your shit. By St. Helen's cross, I wish I had your balls in my hand, instead of a lot of relics. I'd cut them off, and enshrine them in a pig's turd."

The pilgrims crack up, as do we, at Chaucer's brilliantly vivid language, and for the briefest moment it looks as if the pilgrimage stands in danger of falling apart, since the thing that is holding it together is respect for Harry Bailey's authority, and that is now in jeopardy. At this funny but crucial moment the Knight intervenes, and calls upon both Harry Bailey and the Pardoner to make up their quarrel. "No more of this," he insists, "Sir Pardoner, be glad and cheerful. And you, Sir Host, that are so dear to me, kiss the Pardoner, and as we have been, let us laugh and play." At once the men make up their difference, and the pilgrimage continues on its way.

There is yet another tale in which the question of Death figures prominently, and that is the *Monk's Tale*, which consists of a sort of shopping list of heroes and antiheroes, more or less from the time of Lucifer but extending up to fourteenth-century contemporaries of Chaucer as well, those who were great in their day, but were then utterly destroyed. The Monk, who is probably referring back to the *Knight's Tale* when he speaks his own, refers to what he, and many in the Middle Ages (and since) would call a tragedy: a story of those who were "in great prosperity," but "fell into misery, and ended wretchedly." Tragedy for him consists in the fall of a great one from high estate to low, a collapse usually ending in death. Hercules, the mythic hero, and Zenobia, the third-century Queen of Palmyra, Alexander, Julius Caesar, and Cresus all appear, as well as some moderns: Peter, King of Spain, who is known to history as Pedro, King of Castile and León, murdered in 1369, and whose court Chaucer may himself have visited on his 1366 diplomatic mission to Spain; Peter, King of Cyprus, that is, Pierre de Lusignan, well known in England (which he had visited in 1363), killed by three of his own knights in 1369. We really don't know what order Chaucer put these in, or if he was still making up his mind when he died, but the view of death which he develops is not unlike the one which appears in the *Pardoner's Tale*. In both tales it functions almost mechanically, although in the case of the *Pardoner's Tale* its actions seem to be triggered by sin, whereas in the *Monk's Tale* it appears simply like nemesis, destroying good and bad alike for no other reason than it has a mind to do so.

This is not a very lively or interesting way of viewing the course of human life, however, and so once again the Knight intervenes. "Good Sir, no more of this! You've said enough, and more than enough!" A little "heaviness" goes a long way, he tells the Monk. Instead of simply telling how the great fell, he insists, in what we might just call an American turn of phrase, that now he wants to hear a little of the opposite, how a man who was in poverty climbed out of it, became fortunate, and now lives ("abideth") in prosperity. Seeing how things are going, Harry Bailey jumps on the Monk as well: "He speaks of how Fortune covers with a cloud I know not what," he petulantly objects. "It's no remedy to bewail and complain. Your tale is annoying all of us," he adds. "Such talking is not worth a butterfly, for in it there is no disport or game." But the Monk, who knows that his theme has been Death, and believes that he has reached deeper into this great theme than the Knight ever did in his tale, may also have seen a certain appropriateness to the Knight's cowardly intervention, and refuses Harry Bailey's request to tell another tale.

Many reasons have been given for the Knight's interruption of the Monk, but these are really not particularly obscure. A lively and original colloquium published in *Studies in the Age of Chaucer*[6] focused largely upon the putative attack the Monk makes upon the Knight, perhaps partly because critics tend to like it when the pilgrims attack each other, since it seems to offer a rough parallel to what they themselves do. But the pilgrims are not always on the attack: sometimes one tale extends, even completes another, sometimes it offers a different slant on what has just been said. Harry Bailey indeed asks the Monk to "quit," or repay, the Knight, and the Knight, perhaps timorously, may not want to hear him through, but it is a mistake to think that the Host is the only pilgrim who misunderstands the tales he hears. What the Monk really does to the Knight is to raise a curtain behind his tale, one which puts it into another perspective entirely. For if in one way the Monk echoes the Pardoner, in another he echoes the Knight. Fortune cannot be avoided, and seems to cover everything, just as Harry Bailey says. And however hard you try, however great your accomplishments, in the end your fate is to die, and even though, like Theseus and perhaps also the young knights, you may come to terms with your mortality during the course of your life here, in the end you die. If the death of a youth like Arcite seems one violation of the natural order, the death of a great one, or of many great ones, is another, and one that neither Theseus nor the Knight can quite explain. Death may be one with love, whether secular or religious, but it is also other, an absolute difference which, however crudely, inclines many to consider their end.

It is thus not surprising that Chaucer himself did not face death unprepared. At the end of the *Canterbury Tales* there is a short prose passage universally accepted as having come from Chaucer's pen, and usually referred to as "Chaucer's Retraction," though in fact in manuscripts it is simply headed "Here the maker of this book takes his leave," so that really it is his farewell more than anything else.[7] But I myself find it difficult to read this really very moving little work without hearing another text as well, the so-called "Seven Interrogations," questions which a priest would put to a dying Christian to be certain that his theological opinions were orthodox, and that he or she was in a state of grace. Writing in *Death and Burial in Medieval England*, Daniell (36) summarizes them thus: the dying person is asked by a priest (1) whether he or she accepts the Articles of Faith, and the Bible, and rejects all heresy; (2) whether s/he understands that s/he has offended God; (3) whether s/he is sorry for past sins; (4) whether s/he would amend his or her life, given more time; (5) whether s/he forgives his or her enemies; (6) whether s/he would make satisfaction; and (7) whether s/he believes that Christ died for us, that we may not be saved but through Christ's passion, for which we thank him with all our heart. It was only after having satisfied the priest on these questions that the dying person was allowed to receive the final sacrament, Extreme Unction, and take Communion for the last time, the Viaticum.

But it may not be a coincidence that Chaucer's "retractions" echo most if not all of the Seven Interrogations. Chaucer does not name the Articles of Faith as such, but an acceptance of gospel teaching and a rejection of error are at the heart of this final little prose work, in which, however traditional the matter may be, the poet evidently speaks in his own voice. In it, Chaucer expresses sorrow and asks pardon for "my giltes," and includes in those his writing and translating of "worldly vanities," which he carefully names, excluding others, however, for which, echoing devout belief, he thanks Christ and the Virgin Mary. He asks that from henceforth unto his life's end they may send him "grace to bewail my giltes and to study the salvation of my soul," and concludes with a prayer for "true contrition, confession and satisfaction," which he asks "through the benign grace of he that is King of kings and priest over all priests, who brought us with the precious blood of his heart." This last detail in particular answers the last specific requirement of the Interrogations that it was Christ's passion which saved us, and for which we thank him with all our heart. Even the fifth requirement, that he forgive his enemies, which is not explicitly present, may resonate in his rejection of those of his works which may lead into sin. But it is certainly possible to believe that Chaucer ended his great work not with a Retraction but with an affirmation of the sort which, in his day at least, all dying Christians would have articulated.

And yet whatever his final and personal accommodation, the fact of death has a powerful and unsettling presence in Chaucer's fictions. It attaches to the young (the *Pardoner's Tale*), to the aging (the *Knight's Tale*), and to the most powerful (the *Monk's Tale*). It is present even when it is unexpected, but it is also a most important part of life, indeed, it becomes a central way of understanding life's aspirations and significance. Even when, as with Arcite's death, it seems to the observer finally inexplicable, it often indicates meanings beyond itself, acknowledging the often painful but sometimes sublime realities of human life, and representing its significance in a way which is, in the end, at the heart of Chaucer's art.

8

Conclusion

Famously unfinished, the *Canterbury Tales* has had as great an influence on the course of English narrative as any work ever written. It is far from the oldest narrative in English literature, which has a very early tradition of vernacular narratives, of which *Beowulf*, composed at least four centuries before the *Canterbury Tales*, is only the best known. Chaucer's great importance lay in the fact that he was first in a generation of established writers of English who engaged narrative for its own sake, irrespective of the demands of cultural, national, or ideological identity, which, nonetheless, informed his work. This freedom from some kinds of external requirement did not make him a more powerful storyteller, but it did open his tales to the influences around him, which are reflected less in his specific allusions to them, though these do occur, than by the interplay between and among the pilgrims, often in the interest of larger themes than those which they consciously engage; the movement away from an idealized depiction of character, while at the same time sometimes preserving it carefully, particularly when it could be used to good effect; and a growing attention to secular detail, not all of it important to the narrative.

Intellectual inquisitiveness, but also playfulness, is at the heart of Chaucer's best work, as they are in all good fictions. But his playfulness does not indicate a lack of seriousness ("full many a serious thing is said in jest"), though it is related to a finally comic view of life not unlike Dante's, which involves appearances which do not always deceive; exits and entrances which encode the most important of choices; and an unyielding sense of time which is, however, at least partly the author's to dispose of. It is true, of course, that against Chaucer's new, plastic aesthetic, stand the hard realities, and I have named them as I have found them, Love and Death, Visions and Constructions, Others and God.

My purpose here has been to begin to make Chaucer's *Canterbury Tales* familiar to you, so that you can read it with greater pleasure, dissenting, no doubt, from some, from much, of what I have written, but awake to the work's wandering but attentive scope; to its intricate but skeptical depth; and to its finally irreducible author.

9

Which Tale Was That? A Summary of the *Canterbury Tales*

What follows is a short description of the plots which make up the *Canterbury Tales*, together with an indication of the nature of the work as a whole. The summaries are intended to help distinguish the tales, and touch upon, but (note well) do not develop the connections between and among them. I have kept Chaucer's Middle English spelling of personal, though not of place, names, but have added the Modern English in parentheses where I thought it useful.

The order of the tales has traditionally been seen as authorial, though it is now impossible to say whether the organization of the tales into the ten fragments which appear in manuscripts was also Chaucer's, left among his papers at the time of his death, or was developed by early scribal practice. I have indicated by Roman numerals which tales belong to which fragments, following an order found both in the important Ellesmere MS and in very many editions of the *Canterbury Tales*; I have also listed capital letters which reflect an earlier attempt to order the tales by the Chaucer Society. If the connections between and among tales in individual fragments is often obvious, the fragments connections are less so, but I have noted the familiar "Bradshaw Shift" in Fragment VII (Group B2), which is followed in a few modern editions.

Fragment I (Group A)

General Prologue   The *Canterbury Tales* begins in the Tabard Inn, in Southwark, where a group of 30 pilgrims meet by chance, and agree to travel together to Canterbury. The Host of the inn, Herry Bailey (Harry Bailly), offers to travel with them "at my own cost," acting as guide and judge of the tales he bids them tell. He suggests that each of the 30 pilgrims tell two tales going to Canterbury, two tales coming back, and that the teller of the best of these receive a dinner at his inn on their return, for which the whole company would pay. He will choose the best tale by considering both meaning and pleasure, "best sentence," and "most solaas." The following day they set off, and shortly thereafter, whether by chance, luck or fate, the Knight draws the lot to begin the contest.

Knight's Tale   The longest, most complex narrative in the *Canterbury Tales*, the *Knight's Tale* recounts a romance in which Palamon (identified throughout with Venus) and Arcite (identified throughout with Mars) contend with each other for Emelya (who follows Diana). It is set in the ancient world, and begins when Theseus, victoriously returning to Athens with Ypolita (Hippolita), formerly Queen of the defeated Amazons, now his wife, and Emelya (Emily) her daughter, is prevailed upon by supplication of the wives and daughters of the men whom he has killed and whose bodies he has left unburied to attack Creon, the tyrant of Thebes. After the battle, the young noble cousins Palamon and Arcite are found alive in a pile of bodies, but Theseus knows them to be his sworn enemies and imprisons them for life in Athens. Years pass, and the young knights fall in love with Emelya, whom they see, unknown to her, walking in her garden; as a result of their mutual infatuation they become sworn enemies. Arcite is released through a friend's influence, but forbidden upon pain of death ever to return to Athens. But a year or two later, through the help of the god Mercury, he does return, accepting a lowly position as Emelya's page; subsequently Palamon escapes from prison, and, through fate, accident, or providence, the two meet in the forest, and fight. While they are thus engaged Theseus arrives with a hunting party which includes Emelya and Ypolita, and the women prevent Theseus from having the two executed. Instead he decrees a tournament in a year's time, to which each knight will bring 100 knights and champions, carefully described. The night before battle Theseus gives a great feast, and afterwards the knights and Emelya pray to their respective gods. In the heavens, Saturn promises Venus that her knight shall not fail to win his prize. On the next day, one knight wins, but the other is killed in the moments following his victory by what appears to the onlookers a freak accident, but which is really the direct intervention of the gods. The other knight wins Emelya's hand, but, by Theseus'direction, they may not be married until a year has passed.

Miller's Prologue   After the Knight has told his tale the Host turns to the Monk and bids him "quite" or repay the Knight for his tale, but is interrupted by the drunken Miller, who insists that he will instead, and rejects the Host's attempts to quiet him. He has just begun to speak when he is interrupted by the Reeve, but he insists on continuing, and at the end of his Prologue a narrative voice apologizes for his and the Reeve's tales, and warns the reader "not to make earnest of game."

Miller's Tale   A riotous reprise of the *Knight's Tale*, the *Miller's Tale* tells of the romance between Nicholas, an Oxford student, and Alison, the wife of the old, innocent, and somewhat dim carpenter named John with whom he is lodging. New to Chaucer's version of this traditional tale is the character of Absolon (Absolom), the fastidious and squeamish parish clerk, who is also in love with Alison, though she prefers Nicholas. Nicholas convinces John that a second flood is about to occur, and that he, Alison, and Nicholas should spend the night in three kneading tubs secured with ropes to the rafters, so as to escape drowning when the flood comes. The ruse allows Nicholas and Alison to leave the tubs and make love, but as they are doing so Absolon appears below their window, seeking Alison. Invited to climb up to the window for a kiss, he receives a fart instead, but when he returns with a hot iron to repay the trick, he instead brands Nicholas, who cries out "Water," whereupon John awakens and cuts the ropes which are holding his tub to the ceiling, but since there is no flood below he falls to the floor and breaks his arm. The commotion awakens neighbors, who rush in to see what is amiss, but the sight of the old husband and young wife explains all, and they fall about laughing at poor John.

Reeve's Prologue   Osewold the Reeve objects to the Miller's tale because he was once a carpenter, and complains about being an old man, listing the vices of the old as boasting, lying, anger, and greed, though admitting that his own youthful lusts have almost played out. The Host points out that it is about 7:30 AM, and that they are now at Greenwich, about five miles from London.

Reeve's Tale   The Reeve tells the tale of Symkin, a miller in

Trumpington, near Cambridge, who lives with his wife, a beautiful young daughter, Malyne, and an infant, and who is known for cheating his clients. He is confronted by two Cambridge undergraduates from King's Hall, who come from the north of England, Aleyn (Allen) and John, who bring the college's grain to be ground, and set out not to be fooled. The miller understands what's going on, and as they prepare to resist his plans he unties their horse, which gallops away, pursued by the two clerks. While they are away he steals some of their flour and directs his wife to bake a cake with it. The two students then return to the mill to spend the night, their college gates now being shut against them. During the night, one student leaves his bed to sleep with the miller's daughter, while the other, by a ruse involving a moved cradle, causes his wife to enter his bed. Daylight brings discovery and attempted retribution, but thanks in part to the daughter's complicity and the wife's misdirected blow, the students escape with flour and cake both.

Cook's Prologue   The Cook laughs at the Reeve's tale, and the Host calls on him to tell the next tale, but when he chides him for some of his practices, the Cook warns the Host that he will tell a tale about a Host before he is done.

Cook's Tale   The Cook begins the (uncompleted) tale of Perkyn (Perkin) Revellour, the idle and undisciplined London apprentice who loves the tavern better than his master's shop, and loves as well dancing, dice, and lovemaking. His long-suffering master realizes that he is better off without him, and turns him out, whereupon Perkin moves in with a fellow thief whose wife keeps a shop and sells her favors on the side, but at this point the tale breaks off.

Fragment II (Group B1)

Introduction to the Man of Law's Tale   The Host indicates that it is now about 10:00 AM, moralizes, and calls upon the Man of Law, who begins by complaining that Chaucer, since his youth, has told in poetry so many tales in "such English as he can" that he will now speak in prose (he doesn't). He then utters a *Prologue* which complains about the evils and rigors of poverty, concluding by saying that he will tell a tale he learned from a merchant.

Man of Law's Tale   The Host points out that it is 10:00 A.M. on the morning of April 18, and bids the pilgrims use their time wisely. The Man of Law tells the tale of a Roman emperor's daughter, Dame Custance (Constance), who is sent to marry a Syrian sultan, who has heard of her beauty through merchants and offered conversion for her hand. When she arrives, however, her new mother-in-law has prepared a wedding banquet at which her son and his Christian supporters are killed, and has Custance put out to sea in a rudderless boat, which, after three years, protected all the time by God, arrives in Northumberland, in England. There she marries (and has a child by) by King Alla, whom she converts, but whose mother, while her son is away, puts her to sea again in a rudderless boat, in which she has a dramatic encounter with a thief, after which she drifts for five years until she meets, at sea, the Roman Emperor, returning home after having taken his vengeance in Syria for his daughter's treatment there: with him she returns to Rome, where she subsequently meets again her husband Alla, who has come on pilgrimage to do penance for having slain his wicked mother. He sees a family likeness in Custance's son, and the family is reunited. After some years he dies, and Constance spends her final years in doing good deeds.

Epilogue   The Host calls upon the Parson to speak next, but when he is reproved for swearing he suggests that the Parson is a Lollard, a follower of John Wyclif and by extension a heretic, which causes the Shipman (or some other pilgrim, the manuscripts differ as to who interrupts) to offer to speak next.

Fragment III (Group D)

Wife of Bath's Prologue   Dame Alice of Bath delivers a very long prologue which relies on experience to examine the Christian teaching on marriage, and recounts her married life with five husbands, three old, rich, and good, whom she abused; a fourth who kept a lover, and whose life she made a purgatory, and finally her last, Jankyn, a young husband whom she loved dearly, in spite of his anti-feminist learning. She notes that now she is looking for a sixth, and compares, among other things, virginity and wedded life. At the end of her Prologue the Friar interjects that "This is a long preamble of a tale," but he is in turn interrupted by the Summoner, and the two threaten each other with the tales to come.

Wife of Bath's Tale The Wife of Bath tells a tale in which a young knight of King Arthur's court who has raped a peasant is, at the king's direction, sentenced by the queen and other ladies to discover what it is that women most desire. His quest is long and unavailing until he sees more than 24 ladies dancing, but they vanish when he approaches them, leaving only an ugly old woman who promises to tell him what he seeks, if he will promise to do the next thing she asks of him. He agrees and returns to court, where the old woman's answer proves correct: but she demands his hand in marriage, and the court constrains him to keep his word. On his wedding night he complains bitterly, but the old woman teaches him that contrary to his pride, Christ directs that we claim our nobility from him, and then offers him an important choice, which defines the ending of the tale.

Friar's Prologue The Friar commends the Wife, and notes that since they are speaking in game they need not cite church authorities, but that he will now clobber the Summoner. The Host warns him to think of his position in society ("your estate") before doing so, but the Summoner insists he speak his will, and that he will pay him back.

Friar's Tale The Friar tells the tale of an ecclesiastical officer called a summoner whose duty it is to summon those called to the Archdeacon's court. This summoner serves a particularly severe Archdeacon, and meets on his travels a yeoman dressed in green, from the north, who turns out to be a fiend from hell. The two ride together, each searching for what he can legitimately take, though unlike the summoner, the fiend is constrained by intentionality, that is, the person cursing must mean what he or she says, and the wrong done must be intended. They observe a man with a cart first damning, then blessing, his horse, but when they come to an old woman's house the summoner demands a bribe to excuse her from an accusation which he has invented, so that she curses him in terms which meet the requirements of theology, and the fiend carries him off to hell.

Summoner's Prologue The Summoner begins with a brief story of a friar who has a vision which shows him hell; when he wonders where all the friars are, the angel who is conducting him bids Satan lift up his tail. Satan does so, and the friars, who live in his ass, swarm out like bees, but then return again. The friar awakens from his vision in terror of what he has seen.

Summoner's Tale   The Summoner replies with a tale about a friar who has been assigned territory in Holderness for preaching and begging, and who has ingratiated himself with a noble household, claiming both an intimacy with the wife and, with false humility, a revelation that a recently deceased child has gone to heaven. He has come to extract a generous donation – he stresses that what he receives must be divided between him and the 12 friars in his convent – from Thomas, the now ill head of the house, whom he first reproves for having spread his charity too widely, and then for the deadly sin of anger. Thomas promises a donation provided the friar promises to share it with his 12 brothers: he agrees, but putting his hand where Thomas directs him receives only a fart. He explodes with anger, and is immediately shown the door. At the next house he pedantically wonders how he can divide the fart he has received as he has promised. Thereupon a squire, for a promised reward, proposes that he be placed at the center of a cartwheel, with a brother friar at the end of each spoke. He should then emit a fart, and each friar would receive his part of it.

Fragment IV (Group E)

Clerk's Prologue   The Host calls upon the shy Clerk of Oxford to tell "some merry thing," avoiding lenten sermons and the high style of rhetoric. The Clerk agrees, since he is under the Host's authority, and says he will tell a tale of that worthy clerk Francis Petrarch, whom he praises.

Clerk's Tale   The Clerk, responding to the Wife of Bath, tells the semi-allegorical tale of patient Griselde (Griselda), married, at the urging of "the people" and the agreement of her father, the peasant Janicula, to a marquis named Walter, who first seems to love her as much as the people do. Soon after their wedding a daughter is born, then, four years later, a boy. Walter tests Griselde's love of him first by the pretended but apparent murder of their daughter, in whose death Griselde acquiesces, because it is Walter's will, blessing her daughter, and asking the putative murderer only that she be carefully buried. Two years after their son's birth, Walter announces it will be necessary also for their son to die, giving as his reason that the people object to being ruled by one with peasant's blood; again

Griselde agrees, asking only his burial. Wondering at his wife's patience, and certain that she loves their children, six years later Walter claims, with the use of counterfeit Papal bulls, that the Pope and the people too have directed him to take another wife, and desires Griselde to prepare his house to receive her, and then to be gone, leaving as poor as she came. Again Griselde agrees, but this is the last of her tests, and the new wife is revealed to be her still-living daughter, and her son and her position are now likewise restored. At the end Chaucer or the Clerk speaks an *Envoy* which warns that the tale is not to be read literally, and calls upon women to defend themselves. The Host, missing the point, wishes that his wife had heard the tale.

Merchant's Prologue   The Merchant complains about his wife, "the worst that may be," though he has been married only two months, and proceeds to tell his tale.

Merchant's Tale   The Merchant tells the tale of old, rich January, aged over 60, a Knight, and Fresh May, his young bride of lower rank, whose marriage is debated by honest Justinus, who opposes it, and sycophantic Placebo, who does not. A disastrous wedding night leaves May hoping for more, which she finds in the person of Damyan (Damion), a young squire whose lovesickness she discovers when, sent by January, she visits him to see if he is well. January's blindness facilitates their trysts, which take place in a locked garden to which they obtain, through a wax impression, a duplicate key. Engaged in lovemaking in a pear tree, they are spied by Pluto and Proserpyne (Proserpina), the first of whom restores January's sight, so that he can see wife and squire making love, but the second of whom supplies May with a ready answer to calm, even with the evidence of what he sees, her husband's suspicions.

Epilogue   The Host again complains about both women in general and also his wife, a shrew with "a heap of vices more."

Fragment V (Group F)

Introduction to the Squire's Tale   The Host calls upon the Squire to tell his tale.

Squire's Tale   The Squire tells a tale set in Tartary, in which King Cambuskan is holding a feast on his March birthday, when an unknown knight enters with a flying brass horse, which can take its rider anywhere in 24 hours; a magic mirror, which reveals any adversary of the king or his kingdom, and which also shows who is his friend, who his foe; a gold ring, which allows the wearer to understand, and to speak, the language of birds, and also to know which herbs will provide good medicine; and a naked sword, which can cut through all armor, and whose wound cannot be healed except by being stroked with the sword which inflicted it. The horse vanishes, but mirror and ring are given to Candace, the king's daughter, who thus hears the story of a female falcon, who has been spurned in love. Great adventures are promised, but here the tale breaks off, as the Squire is interrupted by the Franklin, who praises his wit, but excuses him from a tale which has become all but unmanageable, and offers to tell a tale in his place.

Franklin's Prologue   The Franklin, a middle-class landowner who rides with the Man of Law, describes the Breton Lay and says he will tell one, but warns that he is unsophisticated and never learned rhetoric, and so will speak "bare and plain."

Franklin's Tale   The Franklin recounts a Breton lay in which a Knight Arveragus leaves his loved wife Dorigen for two years in England, there to seek honor in arms. During this time Dorigen is approached by a young squire, Aurelius, who pledges a love which he knows to be hopeless, only to hear Dorigen set him an apparently impossible task: remove all the black rocks from the shipwrecking coast of Brittany, so that Arveragus can return to her in safety. With the help of a magician friend to whom he has promised £1,000, Aurelius manages not exactly to remove the rocks, but to have the ocean level raised, so that the rocks appear to have been removed. Dorigin is shocked, and utters a lamentation to Fortune, listing 22 women who have killed themselves in similar circumstances. Aurelius then returns. Arveragus seeks to claim his reward, and Dorigen is torn between her vow to Aurelius and her love of her just-returned husband. Arveragus thereupon agrees that she can fulfill her vow so long as she does not tell anyone that she has done so, but when Aurelius hears of Arveragus' apparent generosity, he forgives Dorigen her promise, only to be himself forgiven the £1,000 he has promised the magician for his work. The tale ends by asking which of these three men was the most generous.

Fragment VI (Group C)

*This is the so-called "Floating Fragment," which contains neither geographi-
cal references nor obvious connection to any of the other tales. Its designation
as Group C was predicated upon the "Bradshaw Shift" (see Fragment VII,
below), so as to allow it to follow immediately the reconstituted Group B1–B2.*
Physician's Tale   The Physician speaks without Preface or Introduction, telling a tale from the Roman historian Livy concerning a knight,
Virginius and, graced by Nature, his beautiful daughter Virginia, who
is loved by the evil judge Apius, who, on the basis of a false witness
supplied by his servant Claudius, claims Virginia as his slave. Her con-
demnation to slavery assured, her father insists there is no alternative
to death, and she agrees. He thereupon kills his daughter, which causes
the people to rise up against Apius, whom they throw into prison,
where he kills himself. Claudius is sentenced to be hanged, but
Virginius causes his punishment to be reduced to banishment.
Introduction to the Pardoner's Tale   The Host is moved by the
Physician's tale and turns to the Pardoner for a merrier one, and the
Pardoner agrees, but wants to stop for a drink and a cake first. Other
pilgrims object, and call for a moral tale, and the Pardoner agrees,
but insists he have a drink while he is thinking.
Pardoner's Prologue   The Pardoner describes the way he preaches
in church, showing his credentials, speaking a few words of Latin,
showing his putative relics which he says have the power to cure
farmyard animals, warning off those with great sins or who are
cuckolds, and telling many old tales, since "ignorant people love old
tales." He reveals that his intention is to win money, not to correct
sin, but preaches that cupidity is the root of evil.
Pardoner's Tale   Pardoner tells an extended *exemplum*, a short narrative told in a sermon to point a moral, in this case that greed is the
root of all evil. Three riotous young men, much given to gambling,
whorehouses, drinking, and swearing, learn that Death has recently
slain one of their friends, and set out to kill him. They rudely ask
directions from an enigmatic old man who is seeking either Death
or someone who will change his youth for his age, who sends them
along a crooked way to an oak tree where they find eight bushels of
gold coins, a number divisible by two, but not by three. They forget
their quest, and the older two send the youngest off to town to buy

bread and wine. When he returns they murder him, as they have agreed between them, so as to cheat him of his share; then they drink the wine he has brought, but he has had a like impulse, and two of the three bottles have been poisoned.

Fragment VII, Group B2

Fragment B2 has sometimes been placed immediately following Fragment B1 as the result of a suggestion made in the middle of the nineteenth century by the medieval liturgist and textual critic Henry Bradshaw (the "Bradshaw Shift"), who pointed out that doing so would regularize the geographical references in the work, placing a reference to Rochester (Monk's Tale, line 3116) before a reference to Sittingbourne (Wife of Bath's Tale, line 847). But it is no less possible that Chaucer shifted the tales himself, moving the Wife of Bath's Tale, and those tales associated with it, forward, as he developed the Wife of Bath's character, role, and importance, then assigning her first tale to the Shipman. If that was what happened, in due course he probably would have altered the references to place-names, much as he might have altered the suggestion in the General Prologue that each pilgrim would tell four tales. Placing the tales in the present (Ellesmere MS) order, if that was what he did, was both dramatic and artistically effective, and had the effect of positioning the more secular tales (apart from the Man of Law's) towards the beginning of the work, and moving away from them, to tales which, as a general rule, are more moral and religious.

Shipman's Tale The Shipman speaks without Preface or Introduction, telling the tale of a merchant living in Saint Denis, north of Paris, who is visited by a trusted family friend, Daun John, a monk who is too familiar with his wife, who privately tells him she desperately needs 100 francs. On the third day of the visit the merchant shuts himself away in his counting-house to plan a business trip to Bruges, but before he departs Daun John asks the loan of 100 francs for a week or two in order to buy certain beasts for his monastery. The merchant agrees, but while he is away the monk uses the money to pay for a night of lovemaking with the merchant's wife instead. The merchant, who had been forced by the high prices in Bruges to borrow additional money on a short-term note from creditors in Paris, sees the monk when he returns to Paris to repay it, and the monk tells him that he has repaid the loan to his wife. When, after a night of lovemaking, he taxes his wife with the repayment she curses the monk, and insists that she had not known that there was a loan involved, and thought the money was a contribution toward the hospitality he had often enjoyed there, and was hers to do with as she liked. When she tells him she will not repay him except in bed he sees that he has no choice but to agree, so he forgives her the debt, but urges her in the future not to spend so freely, but to keep their goods better.

At the end the Host praises the tale, and calls upon the Prioress.

Prioress's Prologue   The Prioress begins by invoking "O Lord, our Lord," who is praised both by men of dignity and by children, and promises to tell a tale in his praise, and in that of his mother, whose virtues are inexpressible, but which she will celebrate in the sort of tale a young child might tell, since her knowledge is so limited.

Prioress's Tale   The Prioress tells a tale of a type known as the "Miracles of the Virgin," which is set in an Asian city and concerns a seven-year-old Christian boy who walks daily through the Jewish quarter on his way to school. Hearing the *Alma redemptoris* sung by his older classmates, he learns that the song is in praise of Mary, and resolves to learn and sing it on the way to and from school. At the urging of Satan the Jews hire a murderer to kill the boy and throw his body into the town sewer. When he does not return that night his mother is frantic, and at first light seeks him everywhere. Through God's grace the boy is found singing the *Alma redemptoris* loudly, even though his throat has been cut. The Christians call the Provost, and the boy's body is brought in procession to an abbey, while the Provost orders that all the Jews who knew of the murder be at once drawn by wild horses and hung. The boy's body is carried to the main altar where a mass is celebrated, the boy singing *Alma redemptoris* all the while. The abbot asks the boy how he can sing since his throat is cut, and the boy answers that Mary has laid a grain upon his tongue, and will take him to heaven when it is removed. The abbot removes the grain and the boy dies. The Christians build him a marble tomb, and the tale ends with a prayer to Young Hugh of Lincoln, also believed murdered by "cursed Jews," and in Chaucer's time worshipped as a saint.

Prologue to Chaucer's Tale of Sir Thopas   The Prioress's tale has made the pilgrims "sober," so to lighten the mood the Host turns to Chaucer, jokes with him, and calls for "a tale of mirth." Chaucer agrees, but protests ignorance, and says that he can only offer "a rhyme I learned long ago."

Chaucer's Tales: The Tale of Sir Thopas and the Tale of

Melibee   Chaucer tells a brilliant comic parody of a tail-rime romance, popular in the fourteenth century, though the Host fails to recognize that it as a parody, and interrupts the tale before he can finish it. As it stands, it tells of Sir Thopas, an effete but adventurous knight who dresses a little too well, follows pursuits, like wrestling and archery, which few knights do, seeks an elf-queen as his lover and runs away from a battle with a giant called Sir Oliphaunt (Elephant), but just as the narrative is becoming interesting, the Host interrupts and asks for another tale.

Chaucer agrees, and follows with the long prose *Tale of Melibee*, a form of wisdom literature in which three "adversaries," subsequently identified as the World, the Flesh and the Devil, attack Melibee's wife Prudence, and mortally wound his daughter, Sophie ("Wisdom"), though the tale subsequently alludes to Sophie's possible resuscitation. Melibee, a powerful, proud, and rich young man, seeks to apprehend and punish his adversaries, but fails to understand that they are an extension of his own sinfulness. When the guilty parties are apprehended and brought before him for judgment, he seeks advice, and finds his own antifeminism ("women are wicked") transformed by the teachings of Prudence, who cites Christ's birth, and his appearance after his resurrection to Mary Magdalene, as proof of women's virtue. Prudence defers to her husband in many things, but manages him effectively, sometimes with the appearance of anger. Finally moved by her advice, Melibee ignores those calling for vengeance and war in favor of those who urge forgiveness, and shows mercy to those who have wronged him. The tale addresses both public and private policy (indeed, Melibee's threat to exile his adversaries attributes to him kingly powers), and warns as effectively against war as it does against personal revenge, suggesting that moderation and self-control play a part in each.

Monk's Prologue   The Host shows, in his appreciation of Chaucer's tale and his sexist remarks about his wife, that he has failed to understand it, alludes to the fact that they have come as far as Rochester, and calls upon the Monk, whom he had first called upon after the Knight had finished, to tell the next tale, but he does so in an offhand, discourteous way which refers to the Monk's sexuality, vocation, and appearance. The Monk listens patiently, and offers to tell "a tale, or two, or three," promising next a life of St. Edward, but first some tragedies, tales of those who were in great prosperity but fell from high degree into misery, and ended wretchedly. They do indeed challenge the Knight's chivalric heroism, and he notes that he has a hundred such in his cell.

Monk's Tale   The monk recounts an apparently unstructured and possibly interpolated series of medieval tragedies, including those in the *De casibas* tradition, short *exempla* of great and famous people who fell from high estate to their destruction. The accounts involve biblical examples, like Lucifer, Adam, Nebugodonosor (Nebuchadnezzar), Balthasar, and Sampson; ancient examples, like Alexander, Julius Caesar, Anthiochus, and Cenobia (Zenobia); mythological Hercules; and modern examples, like Peter of Spain (King Petro of Castile and Leòn), Hugelino (Ugolio) of Pisa, Bernabò, Visconte of Milan, and Peter, King of Cyprus. The order of the short accounts, which differs among the manuscripts, is still the subject of scholarly debate, and is of some importance, since the *Monk's Tale* ends when the Knight interrupts it, and the Knight may possibly have done so because of the Monk's literary treatment of Peter of Cyprus, under whom the Knight formerly served.

Nun's Priest's Prologue   The Knight's interruption is at once supported by the Host, who objects that the tales show the powerful role of Fortune, but without any sport or game, and calls upon the Monk to tell a tale about hunting, which the Monk refuses to do. The Host then calls upon the priest who rides with the two nuns to tell a tale, subjecting him to a certain amount of anticlerical disrespect as well.

Nun's Priest's Tale   The tale told by the priest who rides with the Prioress and the Second Nun is one of Aesop's fables, and recounts a story which takes place in the farmyard of a poor widow, who has little but makes do with what she has. It concerns her rooster Chauntecleer, who has a dream in which a beast like a hound, but yellow-red of color, with black-tipped ears and tail, and with a small snout and fierce eyes, tries to seize his body. In a reversal of the usual Aesopic pattern, his favorite wife Pertelote laughs at the dream ("Take a laxative," she advises), but Chauntecleer condescendingly dismisses her scorn by citing numerous learned sources which show dreams can indeed be prophetic and should be taken seriously – but then ignores his own, and shortly thereafter encounters Daun Russell the fox, who is seeking chickens in the farmyard. Encouraged by the fox, who claims to be his friend, to sing, he closes his eyes and does so, only to be seized by the fox and carried off. Chased by all the farmworkers, the fox unthinkingly responds to Chauntecleer's advice that he call back to those in pursuit, but as soon as he opens his mouth Chauntecleer nimbly leaps from his mouth and flies up into a tree. From there he rejects the fox's advice to come down, saying that he will not be misled again by flattery when he should be alert, and cursing himself if he is fooled more than once. The fox calls for bad luck to those who are so ungoverned that they speak when they should keep still. The tale ends with a warning that there is a moral to this tale which runs deeper than the action.

Epilogue The tale is followed in nine manuscripts with a problematic anticlerical passage which alludes to the Nun's Priest's frustrated sexuality and physical strength. It repeats lines and images found in the Monk's *Prologue*, and some scholars now believe that Chaucer canceled the passage after he developed the portrait of the Monk. If he did so, he equally may have been cultivating a somewhat more respectful presentation of the Nun's Priest than the one he first intended, perhaps because of the seriousness of the themes realized in his tale.

Fragment VIII (Group G)

Second Nun's Prologue The (unnamed) Nun who rides with the Prioress (the "Second Nun") begins her Prologue with a warning against spiritual idleness, against which she contrasts spiritual busyness, with which she will characterize the virgin martyr St. Cecilia. She also offers an Invocatio to Mary, citing St. Bernard and asking for Mary's help in the tale she is about to tell, also warning that faith without works is dead. She then offers a series of possible etymologies of the name Cecilia, derived from the life which Brother Jacob of Genoa wrote of her.

Second Nun's Tale The Second Nun's tale is a saint's life, the *passio* (since she was martyred, otherwise a *vita*) of the Roman noblewoman St. Cecile (Cecilia), who warns her husband, the Roman officer Valerian, on their wedding night, that her virginity is guarded by an angel, and that if he goes 3 miles from Rome he will have proof. Valerian does as he is bid, and there meets Pope Urban I, and subsequently an old man dressed in white, who carries a book on which some important words are inscribed. Profoundly moved, he converts to Christianity, and returns home where he finds not only Cecile but also an angel with two crowns, one of white lilies (for chastity), the other of red roses (for martyrdom). Soon after Valerian converts his brother and fellow-officer Tiburce, but the brothers are arrested and, encouraged in their steadfastness by Cecile, martyred. Their teaching, death, and the salvation of their souls is observed and piously reported by their fellow-officer Maximus, whom the cruel judge Almachius martyrs for his witness. Cecile buries the bodies, and effects many conversions, but not long thereafter she is herself arrested and brought before Almachius, whom she bests in dispute, but who orders her execution. The executioner fails, with three strokes of his axe, to sever her head, and must therefore by statute desist. Though in pain, Cecile preaches, distributes her goods, and dedicates her house for a church until she dies, three days later. Pope Urban recovers and buries her body, and the text reveals that her house is now the Church of St. Cecile, in Trastevere, Rome, which is still in use.

Canon's Yeoman's Prologue   The Pilgrims are now at Boughton under Blee, about five miles from Canterbury, when they are overtaken by two men, a Canon dressed in black and his servant, a Yeoman, riding hard, who seek to join their company for the last leg of the trip. The Host senses that something is wrong, and seeks to draw the Yeoman out, asking whether the Canon can tell a tale or two, and speaking to the Yeoman courteously, as though he were an equal, not a social inferior. The Canon seeks to intervene and prevent his Yeoman from continuing what is becoming a conversation, but when he sees that he cannot he gallops away "for sorrow and shame," after which the Yeoman agrees to speak freely about their business, which was alchemy, the attempt to turn base metals into silver or gold.

Canon's Yeoman's Tale   The Canon's Yeoman's tale concerns many aspects of alchemy, founded on his recent experience with the alchemist Canon. It begins with an account of the false and deceptive ways in which alchemists dupe their victims, whether by hiding the gold they pretend to produce in the hollow of a stick with which they stir their formula, or simply by keeping it up their sleeve. It then turns to the case of one victim in particular, a wealthy chantry priest, deceived by an alchemist-canon with the usual tricks (a lump of coal and then a hollowed-out stick in which silver has been concealed), who pays the canon £40 for the recipe. The canon leaves town, the recipe fails to work, and the tale ends with a warning that no man who makes God his adversary will ever come to the philosopher's stone.

Fragment IX (Group H)

Manciple's Prologue   The pilgrims are now at Harbledown, known locally as "Bob-up-and-down," only two miles from Canterbury, when the Host notices that the Cook is asleep on his horse, obviously the result of too much drink. Remembering that he has threatened to tell a tale about innkeepers, he decides that this would be a good moment to call upon him to tell his tale. When the Cook objects that he simply cannot do so, the Manciple interposes and offers to tell one in his place, though as he does so he looks at the Cook, and in a brilliant recognition scene sees his inebriation and first reproves, then denounces the now angry Cook, with the result that the Cook falls off his horse. The Host then intervenes, warning the Manciple that Cooks tend to know the secrets not only of innkeepers but also of Manciples, and that it might be in his own best interest not to reprove the poor man so strongly. The Manciple at once agrees, stops his attack, and, producing a flask of wine, offers the Cook a drink. The Host laughs, agrees that it necessity which makes us act, praises good drink, which can turn rancor into sport, and bids the Manciple begin.

Manciple's Tale   The Manciple tells what amounts to a short fable which recounts how the crow, once a fair, white bird who sang beautifully and was beloved by the noble knight and god Phebus (Phoebus) Apollo, came to his present state. Apollo kept his beautiful crow in a cage, and taught it to speak. But when his much loved wife took a lover while Apollo was away the crow reported the affair by singing "Cokkow! Cokkow! Cokkow!" In a fury, Apollo killed his wife, but then turned on the crow, stripping him of his fine song, his ability to speak, even his white feathers. The tale ends with an injunction to guard your tongue, dissemble when necessary, and remember the crow.

Fragment X (Group I)

Parson's Prologue   After the Manciple has finished his tale the day is much advanced, and the Host suddenly announces that the company now only lacks one tale to complete their agreement, so indicating that Chaucer had altered his plan of having each pilgrim tell two tales going and coming, and was now going to end the *Canter-*

bury Tales at Canterbury, having every pilgrim tell but one tale. He then turns to the Parson for his tale, who cites St. Paul and promises a tale in prose which is also a meditation, insisting that, as a southern man, he cannot speak in alliterative verse. The Host and all the company accept his tale, though the Host warns that the sun will soon set, and bids him hasten and be fruitful, "and that in little space."

Parson's Tale   Whether the *Parson's Tale* is Chaucerian or a scribal addition, it is without the fictional and narrative content which characterizes the other tales, and consists largely of an English translation of two separate penitential handbooks by the Dominican friars St. Raymund of Pennaforte and William Peraldus, though other sources have been added. It treats, in the first part, such topics as the six causes which move men to contrition, the nature of the sacrament of Confession, and, in the second part, at impressive length, the seven deadly sins, which are represented as the source for much human misadventure, including much that has appeared in the *Canterbury Tales*. It invokes the Day of Doom, Hell and the afterlife, against which stands Christ who is seen as the only source for true nobility. The third part of the utterance treats satisfaction, including such practices as almsdeeds, fasting, and bodily discipline, and also those things which disturb penance, and the ways in which the fruit of penance is realized. The focus of the work is moral conduct, and correction.

Chaucer's "Retractions"   At the end of the tales there is an overt acknowledgment by Chaucer that Christ, not he, is responsible for anything good which he has written, but that he assumes responsibility for anything which displeases, asking only that its composition be set down to his ignorance, not his will. He lists many of the works he has written, including "The Book of the Lion," which is yet to be discovered, revoking those which concern worldly vanity, including *Troilus*, the *House of Fame*, the *Book of the Duchess*, the *Parliament of Fowls*, and those of the *Canterbury Tales* which incline towards sin, and many a song and lecherous lay. His other, moral, writings he does not revoke, and asks Christ and Mary and all the saints to send him the grace necessary for contrition and salvation, through the grace of him that is king of kings and priest over all priests, who brought us to salvation with the precious blood of his heart.

Notes

Chapter 1: Who Was Geoffrey Chaucer?

1 Derek Pearsall, *The Life of Geoffrey Chaucer*, Blackwell Critical Biographies 1 (Oxford and Cambridge, MA: Blackwell, 1992). See also Pearsall's Presidential Address to the New Chaucer Society, "The Problems of Writing a Life of Chaucer," *Studies in the Age of Chaucer*, 13 (1991), 5–14. I am indebted to Pearsall throughout this chapter for his excellent biography, to which I have often turned. There is so little we actually know about Chaucer's *poetic* career that the temptation is to invent or infer connections and even events. This Pearsall either refuses to do, or at least makes it very clear when he is doing so.

2 Martin M. Crow and Clair C. Olson, eds., *Chaucer Life-Records* (Oxford: Oxford University Press, and Austin: University of Texas Press, 1966). An astonishing record of Chaucer's *public* career, with some implications for his poetic. The single most important publication for any biographical information.

3 W. Rothwell, "The Trilingual England of Geoffrey Chaucer," *Studies in the Age of Chaucer*, 16 (1994), 45–67. A somewhat specialized, but very interesting, study concerning a rarely examined perspective.

4 New Haven and London: Yale University Press, 1979. See also Fyler's chapter "Pagan Survivals" in Peter Brown, ed., *A Companion to Chaucer*, pp. 349–59.

5 H. Ansgar Kelly, "Shades of Incest and Cuckoldry: Pandarus and John of Gaunt," *Studies in the Age of Chaucer*, 13 (1991), 121–40.

6 See James I. Wimsatt, ed., *Chaucer and the Poems of "Ch" in University of Pennsylvania MS French 15* (Woodbridge, Suffolk: D. S. Brewer; London: Rowman and Littlefield, 1982).

7 On the legal and other uncertainties concerning these actions see

Christopher Cannon, "Chaucer and Rape: Uncertainty's Certainties," *Studies in the Age of Chaucer*, 22 (2000), 67–92.

8 *Fourteenth-Century Studies*, ed. L. S. Sutherland and M. McKisack (Oxford: Oxford University Press, 1937, rpt. 1968).

9 Cambridge, MA: Harvard University Press, 1989.

10 "The Order of *The Canterbury Tales*," *Studies in the Age of Chaucer*, 3 (1981), 77–120.

Chapter 2: Gender and Religion, Race and Class

1 Madison: University of Wisconsin Press, 1989.

2 Giovanni Boccaccio, *Famous Women*, ed. and trans. Virginia Brown, I. Tatti Renaissance Library I (Cambridge, MA: Harvard University Press, 2001), C, pp. 427–37. There is an account of the historical Zenobia in Simon Hornblower and Anthony Spawforth, eds., *The Oxford Classical Dictionary*, third edition (Oxford: Oxford University Press, 1996), s.v. Zenobia.

3 New York: Holt, 1926.

4 Respectively, Dartmouth: Dartmouth History Research Group, 1998 and London: HMSO, 1995.

5 London: Duckworth and Athens: University of Georgia Press, 1983.

6 Oxford and Cambridge, MA: Blackwell, 1991.

7 Gerald Morgan, "Boccaccio's *Filocolo* and the Moral Argument of the *Franklin's Tale*," *Chaucer Review*, 20 (1986), 285–306. An article which opens interesting approaches to the tale, and worth reading also for the ideas it can generate.

Chapter 3: Others

1 Aldershot: Scolar Press and Brookfield, VT: Ashgate, 1997.

2 *A Distinction of Stories. The Medieval Unity of Chaucer's Fair Chain of Narratives for Canterbury* (Columbus: Ohio State University Press, 1981).

3 *Chaucer's Knight. The Portrait of a Medieval Mercenary* (Baton Rouge: Louisiana State University Press, 1980).

4 John H. Pratt, "Was Chaucer's Knight Really a Mercenary?," *Chaucer Review*, 22 (1987), 8–27.

5 Madison: University of Wisconsin Press and London: Routledge, 1991. This book has made an important contribution to the new directions which the study of Chaucer has taken in the last decade.

6   See Katherine Little, "Chaucer's Parson and the Specter of Wycliffism," *Studies in the Age of Chaucer*, 23 (2001), 225–63.

7   Oxford: Oxford University Press, 1926; revised edition, New York: Barnes and Noble, 1960.

8   E. Talbot Donaldson, "Chaucer the Pilgrim," *Proceedings of the Modern Language Association (PMLA)*, 69 (1954), 928–36, but often reprinted, and included in Donaldson's *Speaking of Chaucer (*New York: W. W. Norton, 1970), pp. 1–12. It has been frequently responded to, in the first place by John M. Major, "The Personality of Chaucer the Pilgrim," *Proceedings of the Modern Language Association*, 75 (1960), 160–2.

9   New York: Holt, 1926.

10   "Chaucer the Reactionary: Ideology and the General Prologue to *The Canterbury Tales*," *Review of English Studies*, 51 (2000), 523–39. In spite of the reservation I have noted above, this excellent study should be read for its approach and method as for its content, and is a fine example of the new readings which the *Canterbury Tales* is now receiving.

11   In "The Host, the Law, and the Ambiguous Space of Medieval London Taverns," an article in her book *'Of Good and Ill Repute'. Gender and Social Control in Medieval England* (New York and Oxford: Oxford University Press, 1998), pp. 104–23.

12   Trans. E. B. Ashton (New York: Dial Press, 1947).

13   California Studies in the History of Art, XXXII (Berkeley, Los Angeles, and Oxford: University of California Press, 1993).

Chapter 4: Love

1   Cambridge, MA: Harvard University Press, 1915. In 1976 Kittredge's famous study was reprinted with an introduction by B. J. Whiting.

2   New York: Bedford Books of St. Martin's Press, 1996.

3   Yale Studies in English 96 (London: Oxford University Press, New Haven: Yale University Press and New York: Modern Language Association of America, 1942). Almost singlehandedly this book began a new tradition in source studies by comparing the departures from his sources which Chaucer made as a way of determining his artistic intention. It remains a valuable method even today.

4   "The Non-Comic *Merchant's Tale*, Maximianus, and the Sources," *Medieval Studies*, 29 (1967), 1–25. A particularly good example of source study.

5 The Magic in History Series (University Park, Pennsylvania: The Pennsylvania State University Press, 1998).

6   London: Routledge, 1991.

7   "Chaucer and 'Pite'," in *J. R. R. Tolkien, Scholar and Storyteller. Essays in Memoriam*, ed. M. Salu and Robert T. Farrell (Ithaca, NY: Cornell University Press, 1979), pp. 173–203.

8   Hiroaki Sato, "Japanese Love Poems," in *Love in Asian Art and Culture* (Washington, DC: Arthur M. Sackler Gallery, Smithsonian Institution and Seattle and London: University of Washington Press, 1998), pp. 49–69. For a related book on the way Western medieval attitudes appear in the art of the period, see Michael Camille, *The Medieval Art of Love. Objects and Subjects of Desire* (New York: Harry M. Abrams, 1998).

Chapter 5: God

1   "Chaucer's *Parson's Tale* and the Late-Medieval Tradition of Religious Meditation," *Speculum*, 64 (1989), 600–19. There is another interesting study of the Parson by Robert N. Swanson, "Chaucer's Parson and Other Priests," *Studies in the Age of Chaucer*, 13 (1991), 41–80, and of the question of Chaucer and religion by Charles Muscatine, "Chaucer's Religion and the Chaucer Religion," in *Chaucer Traditions. Studies in Honor of Derek Brewer*, ed. Ruth Morse and Barry Windeatt (Cambridge: Cambridge University Press, 1990), pp. 249–62, rpt. *Medieval Literature, Style and Culture. Essays by Charles Muscatine* (Columbia: University of South Carolina Press, 1999), pp. 26–41.

2   For a good explanation of this and of other aspects of the tale see Penn R. Szittya, "The Friar as False Apostle: Antifraternal Exegesis and the *Summoner's Tale*," *Studies in Philology*, 71 (1974), 19–46. The mature work of a young scholar (it was begun in graduate school), the article is generous in its estimation of previous scholarship (which it documents carefully), and, contrary to academic practice, modest in advancing claims for the originality of its own contribution, which is in fact considerable. It is a good article for a beginning Chaucerian to encounter, both for the evident interest of its substance and for the attractive tone of its address.

3   Princeton: Princeton University Press, 1986. Szittya also has described a connection between the *Friar's Tale* and the *Wife of Bath's Tale* in "The Green Yeoman as Loathly Lady: The Friar's Parody of the *Wife of Bath's Tale*," *Proceedings of the Modern Language Association (PMLA)*, 90 (1975), 386–94.

4   These two tales, together with that of the Prioress and the Second Nun, figure in *Chaucer's Religious Tales*, Chaucer Studies XV, ed. C. David Benson and Elizabeth Robertson, (Cambridge: D. S. Brewer, 1990), as the central religious tales in the Canterbury group, a good starting point

for further reflection on Chaucer's religious attitudes. See also John M. Hill's perceptive study, *Chaucerian Belief. The Poetics of Reverence and Delight* (New Haven and London: Yale University Press, 1991).

5   New Haven and London: Yale University Press, 1999.

6   "The Grain of Paradise," *Speculum*, 36 (1961), 302–7.

7   Morton W. Bloomfield makes a point like this one in "The Man of Law's Tale: A Tragedy of Christian Victimization," *Proceedings of the Modern Language Association*, 87 (1972), 384–90, particularly good on the erotic elements in the tale and on its "low and comic" sex, around which the tale's manifestly religious preoccupations move gingerly.

8   "Chaucer's Disgruntled Cleric," *Proceedings of the Modern Language Association*, 78 (1963), 156–62. Broes's reasonable and humane study is very much of the old school, concerned with the issue of the pilgrims' "personality." To see the development, or at least the change, in Chaucer criticism during the intervening period read it against the study by Alcuin Blamiers cited above, ch. 3, n. 10.

9   Princeton: Princeton University Press, 1994. A penetrating reading of the role of gender in the *Canterbury Tales*.

10 Quebec: Les Editions "L'Eclair", 1956, pp. 29–48.

Chapter 6: Visions of Chaucer

1   The bibliography of Dream Visions and (literary) visions generally is not small, and begins with Robert Easting, *Visions of the Other World in Middle English*, Annotated Bibliographies of Old and Middle English Literature, Volume III (Cambridge: D. S. Brewer, 1997). It includes traditional, perceptive studies like A. C. Spearing's still-valuable *Medieval Dream-Poetry* (Cambridge: Cambridge University Press, 1976), and Carolyn P. Collette, *Species, Phantasms, and Images. Vision and Medieval Psychology in the Canterbury Tales* (Ann Arbor: University of Michigan Press, 2001).

2   In "Modern Times: The Discourse of the *Physician's Tale*," *Chaucer Review*, 27 (1993), 387–95.

Chapter 7: Death

1   *Death and Burial in Medieval England, 1066-1550* (London: Routledge, 1997). There are two fascinating studies of late medieval death in Michael Camille, *Master of Death. The Lifeless Art of Pierre Remiet, Illuminator* (New Haven and London: Yale University Press, 1996) and Jean-

Claude Schmitt, *Ghosts in the Middle Ages. The Living and the Dead in Medieval Society*, trans. Theresa Fagan (Chicago: University of Chicago Press, 1998).

2 *Chaucer and the Imagery of Narrative. The First Five Canterbury Tales* (Stanford, CA: Stanford University Press and London: Edward Arnold, 1984). An important book for anyone interested in the relationship of literature and art in this period. Kolve's influence has been important in this area. See further, *Speaking Images. Essays in Honor of V. A. Kolve*, ed. R. F. Yeager and Charlotte C. Morse (Asheville: Pegasus Press at The University of North Carolina at Asheville, 2001).

3 Though there have been scholars who thought so. See, for example, Edward C. Schweitzer, "Fate and Freedom in *The Knight's Tale*," *Studies in the Age of Chaucer*, 3 (1981), 13–45 for a sympathetic reading of Arcite's death as "not only just but poetically inevitable."

4 *Chaucer and the Shape of Creation. The Aesthetic Possibilities of Inorganic Structure* (Cambridge, MA: Harvard University Press, 1967). Important for its treatment of Chaucer's relationship to Gothic art in general and Gothic cathedrals in particular.

5 I have discussed this Buddhist background for this tale and for two other texts (the saint's life "Barlaam and Josaphat" and the play "Everyman") in "Buddhism and Spirituality in Medieval England," in *The Boundaries of Faith. The Development and Transmission of Medieval Spirituality*, Studies in the History of Christian Thought, Volume LXVII (Leiden, New York, and Köln: E. J. Brill, 1996), pp. 31–46. The Buddhist source has been translated in C. H. Tawney, "The Buddhist Original of Chaucer's Pardoner's Tale," *Journal of Philology*, formerly *Cambridge Journal of Philology*, 12 (1883), 202–8, though this is quite a rare journal, and not in every library.

6 Stephen Knight et al., "Colloquium on *The Monk's Tale*," *Studies in the Age of Chaucer*, 22 (2000), 379–440.

7 It is in a sustained tradition of such pieces, which, as usual, Chaucer has adapted to his own requirements. On the tradition see Olive Sayce, "Chaucer's 'Retractions': The Conclusion of the Canterbury Tales and its Place in Literary Tradition," *Medium Aevum*, 40 (1971), 230–48.

Select Bibliography

With a very few exceptions, I have focused this select bibliography upon important books which are concerned more or less exclusively with Chaucer and the *Canterbury Tales*, or in which these topics figure prominently. There is a selected bibliography by John Leyerle and Anne Quick, *Chaucer. A Bibliographical Introduction*, Toronto Medieval Bibliographies 10 (Toronto, Buffalo, and London: Toronto University Press, 1986), though much has been published in the intervening years. What follows is a general guide to books which may prove useful in developing an understanding of Chaucer and the *Canterbury Tales* – or writing papers about them.

Texts, Language, and Bibliography

Although there are many editions of Chaucer now available, the one on which I have relied here both for Chaucer's text (which, however, I have modernized) and for its often valuable notes is *The Riverside Chaucer*, third edition, General Editor Larry D. Benson (Boston: Houghton Mifflin, 1987), though it should be said that the annotation of this edition was undertaken by different scholars, and that its treatment of matters of biography and cultural and intellectual context differ markedly from tale to tale. In 2000 the publisher issued a second edition of the *Canterbury Tales* alone, for the first time in paperback, in which a certain (often limited) amount of updating has taken place, but not all of the editors have reconsidered their earlier positions, and the effect of the revision on Chaucer studies has not been very great. Still, whatever the extent of remaining critical inconsistency, the "Explanatory Notes" to these editions contain a large amount of useful, available, and factual information, to which the student can turn with confidence. These *Riverside* editions can be supplemented by the appearance, tale by tale, of the Variorum Chaucer (Norman: University of Oklahoma Press, still in progress); by B. A. Windeatt, ed., *Troilus and Criseyde* (London and New York: Longman, 1984); and by Helen Phillips and Nick Havely, eds., *Chaucer's Dream Poetry*, Longman Annotated Texts (London and New York: Longman, 1997).

The *Riverside*'s glossary is excellent, but that of most other editions could usefully be supplemented by *A Chaucer Glossary*, ed. Norman Davis et al. (Oxford and New York: Oxford University Press, 1979). Many of the sources Chaucer used are conveniently collected in W. F. Bryan and Germaine Dempster, eds., *Sources and Analogues of Chaucer's Canterbury Tales* (New York: Humanities Press, 1941, reprinted 1958). A new edition is now underway. The *Riverside Chaucer* takes the Ellesmere manuscript as its base text, though there is another manuscript, the Hengwrt Manuscript, which some scholars prefer (at least in some places), and that has been edited by N. F. Blake as *The Canterbury Tales by Geoffrey Chaucer Edited from the Hengwrt Manuscript* (London: Edward Arnold, 1980). Blake also wrote *The Textual Tradition of the Canterbury Tales* (London: Edward Arnold, 1985). But see *contra* Jill Mann, "Chaucer's Meter and the Myth of the Ellesmere Editor," *Studies in the Age of Chaucer*, 23 (2001), 71–107.

If you are or become interested in Chaucer's manuscripts, a lively study by Charles A. Owen, Jr., *The Manuscripts of the Canterbury Tales*, Chaucer Studies XVII (Cambridge: D. S. Brewer, 1990), should not be missed, though it is somewhat controversial. Stephen Partridge has published *The Manuscript Glosses to the Canterbury Tales* (Woodbridge, Suffolk: Boydell and Brewer, 2001). On Chaucer's language as a separate study, Ralph W. V. Elliott, *Chaucer's English*, The Language Library (London: André Deutsch, 1974) and David Burnley, *A Guide to Chaucer's Language* (London: Macmillan, 1983) are still useful, but on no account miss Christopher Cannon, *The Making of Chaucer's English: A Study of Words*, Cambridge Studies in Medieval Literature 39 (Cambridge: Cambridge University Press, 1998), which finds Chaucer's poetic diction "traditional," rejecting the usual idea that Chaucer began a revolution in English poetic diction. On diction see also Thomas W. Ross, *Chaucer's Bawdy* (New York: E. P. Dutton, 1972). Probably the best translation of the *Canterbury Tales* (based on the Ellesmere manuscript) is by David Wright (Oxford and New York: Oxford University Press, 1985), though it is not to all tastes.

Biography

The single most important work which informs any serious attempt to write the life of Geoffrey Chaucer is *Chaucer Life-Records*, ed. Martin M. Crow and Clair C. Olson (Oxford: Oxford University Press and Austin: University of Texas Press, 1966). It is a most important book, which usefully details every known aspect of Chaucer's life for which there is a written record. If it has any limitation it is that its bulk and apparent inclusiveness tend to discourage any conjecture, however reasonable, about Chaucer's life, and there is much about Chaucer's life which we do not know, at least not yet.

Easily the best biography of Chaucer is by Derek Pearsall, *The Life of Geoffrey Chaucer*, Blackwell Critical Biographies 1 (Oxford and Cambridge, MA: Blackwell, 1992), a book to which, alongside the *Life-Records*, I am deeply indebted throughout. Less sentimental than others, it treats with both learning and insight the problems which confront any serious biographer. It has been my constant companion in writing chapter 1, and the instances in which I have departed from Pearsall's judgments (or his dates) are very few. Two other accounts are by Derek Brewer, *A New Introduction to Chaucer*, second edition, Longman Medieval and Renaissance Library (London: Longman, 1998) and Donald R. Howard's almost novelistic *Chaucer. His Life, his Works, his World* (New York: E. P. Dutton, 1987), published in the UK as *Chaucer and the Medieval World* (London: Weidenfeld and Nicolson, 1987), a very readable account, but one which is by no means innocent of conjecture. There is a popular and lively, if highly conjectural, recent biography by Richard West, *Chaucer 1340–1400. The Life and Times of the First English Poet* (London: Constable, 2000).

One other book of great importance for Chaucer's biography is Paul Strohm, *Social Chaucer* (Cambridge, MA and London: Harvard

University Press, 1989). John of Gaunt figures so importantly in Chaucer's life that Anthony Goodman's perceptive biography, *John of Gaunt. The Exercise of Princely Power in Fourteenth-Century Europe* (London: Longman and New York: St. Martin's Press, 1992), is a useful addition as is Nigel Saul's *Richard II*, Yale English Monarchs (New Haven and London: Yale University Press, 1997).

The Meanings of Chaucer's Text

The best recent overview of Chaucer studies and Chaucer criticism is Peter Brown, ed., *A Companion to Chaucer*, Blackwell Companions to Literature and Culture (Oxford and Malden, MA: Blackwell, 2000), a book so useful, from the point of view of literary and historical criticism, and a select bibliography which follows each chapter, that it makes an excellent starting point for virtually any considered study of Chaucer, particularly by a beginning student. The *Companion* consists of the following 29 topics, each allotted its own chapter and author: 1 Afterlife; 2 Authority; 3 Bodies; 4 Chivalry; 5 Christian Ideologies; 6 Comedy; 7 Contemporary English Writers; 8 Crisis and Dissent; 9 France; 10 Games; 11 Genre; 12 Geography and Travel; 13 Italy; 14 Languages; 15 Life Histories; 16 London; 17 Love; 18 Modes of Representation; 19 Narrative; 20 Other Thought-worlds; 21 Pagan Survivals; 22 Personal Identity; 23 Science; 24 Social Structures; 25 Style; 26 Texts; 27 Translation; 28 Visualizing; and 29 Women.

There is a fine historical anthology of critical commentary on Chaucer edited by Derek Brewer, *Chaucer. The Critical Heritage*, 2 vols. (London: Routledge, 1978), though a more recent examination of the effect of Chaucer on modern literature is Steve Ellis's considered but imaginative *Chaucer at Large. The Poet in the Modern Imagination*, Medieval Cultures 24 (Minneapolis and London: University of Minnesota Press, 2000). A good place to start for a tale-by-tale exposition of more recent criticism is Helen Cooper's excellent volume of the Oxford Guides to Chaucer, *The Canterbury Tales*, second edition (Oxford and New York, 1991). Cooper has also published *The Structure of the Canterbury Tales* (London: Duckworth and Athens: University of Georgia Press, 1983). *The Cambridge Chaucer Companion* is edited by Piero Boitani and Jill Mann (Cambridge: Cambridge University

Press, 1986), and contains some excellent general studies, effectively replacing Beryl Rowland, ed., *Companion to Chaucer Studies*, revised edition (Oxford and New York: Oxford University Press, 1979). Corinne Saunders's *Chaucer* (Oxford and Malden, MA: Blackwell, 2001), in the Blackwell Guides to Criticism series, is a very useful edited collection of critical articles.

General critical studies of Chaucer are not as numerous as they once were, but include Donald R. Howard's *The Idea of the Canterbury Tales* (Berkeley, Los Angeles, and London: University of California Press, 1976), Robert M. Jordan, *Chaucer and the Shape of Creation. The Aesthetic Possibilities of Inorganic Structure* (Cambridge, MA: Harvard University Press, 1967), and see also Jordan's *Chaucer's Poetics and the Modern Reader* (Berkeley, Los Angeles, and London: University of California Press, 1987) and Charles Muscatine, *Chaucer and the French Tradition* (Berkeley, Los Angeles, and London: University of California Press, 1957).

More recent general studies tend toward the specific, and include such recent critical, theoretical, and cultural revaluations as Lee Patterson, *Chaucer and the Subject of History* (Madison: University of Wisconsin Press and London: Routledge, 1991), and David Wallace, *Chaucerian Polity. Absolutist Lineages and Associational Forms in England and Italy*, Figurae: Reading Medieval Culture (Stanford, CA: Stanford University Press, 1997), books of great interest and importance, and which set Chaucer in a broadly intellectual and European context.

Judith Ferster, *Chaucer on Interpretation*, Cambridge Studies in Medieval Literature (Cambridge: Cambridge University Press, 1985) and H. Marshall Leicester, Jr., *The Disenchanted Self. Representing the Subject in the Canterbury Tales* (Berkeley, Los Angeles, and London: University of California Press, 1990) both offer philosophical readings of Chaucer which shift interpretation from literary realism to textual construction, though Ferster focuses on phenomenology and hermeneutics.

V. A. Kolve, *Chaucer and the Imagery of Narrative. The First Five Canterbury Tales* (Stanford, CA: Stanford University Press and London: Edward Arnold, 1984) is a more important and more general study than its title suggests, which brilliantly discusses the (often ignored) visual dimension of the *Canterbury Tales*, focusing on the first five tales, but with important implications for the work as a whole.

Class Studies

Some studies now focus on class and class conflict as an organizing principle: see David Aers, *Chaucer, Langland and the Creative Imagination* (London: Routledge, 1980), Peggy Knapp, *Chaucer and the Social Contest* (London and New York: Routledge, 1990), and Paul A. Olson, *The Canterbury Tales and the Good Society* (Princeton: Princeton University Press, 1986). Two Chaucer essays appear in *The Postcolonial Middle Ages*, ed. Jeffrey Jerome Cohn (New York: Palgrave, 2000): John M. Bowers, "Chaucer After Smithfield: From Postcolonial Writer to Imperalist Author," pp. 53–66; and Sylvia Tomasch, "Postcolonial Chaucer and the Virtual Jew," pp. 243–60; the authors write from very different perspectives. This is a still developing, important topic, and one which has by no means been exhausted.

Gender Studies

Many other studies focus on gender, and one of the earliest of these still retains great interest: Carolyn Dinshaw, *Chaucer's Sexual Poetics* (Madison: University of Wisconsin Press, 1989), and has been followed by others; see among many, Jane Chance, *The Mythographic Chaucer. The Fabulation of Sexual Politics* (Minneapolis and London: University of Minnesota Press, 1995), Elaine Tuttle Hansen, *Chaucer and the Fictions of Gender* (Berkeley, Los Angeles, and London: University of California Press, 1992), Anne Laskaya, *Chaucer's Approach to Gender in the Canterbury Tales* (Cambridge: Cambridge University Press, 1995), and especially Susan Crane, *Gender and Romance in Chaucer's Canterbury Tales* (Princeton: Princeton University Press, 1994). Even more recently, the development of studies in masculinity has been aided by the valuable collection *Masculinities in Chaucer. Approaches to Maleness in the Canterbury Tales and Troilus and Criseyde*, ed. Peter G. Beidler, Chaucer Studies XXV (Cambridge: D. S. Brewer, 1998). Peter Beidler is also the editor of a valuable edition of the *Wife of Bath's Tale* which treats its biographical and historical context, and contains essays which approach it from five different critical perspectives (New York: Bedford Books of St. Martin's Press, 1996). There is a good survey of modern Chaucer criticism by S. H. Rigby: *Chaucer in Context. Society, Allegory and Gender*, Manchester Medieval Studies (Manchester: Manchester University Press, 1996).

But in some ways the theoretical beginning of many recent studies lies in the pioneering work of two British scholars: Helen Cooper, already cited, and Jill Mann, author, among other works, of *Chaucer and Medieval Estates Satire. The Literature of Social Classes and the General Prologue to the Canterbury Tales* (Cambridge: Cambridge University Press, 1973) and *Geoffrey Chaucer*, Feminist Reading Series (Hemel Hempstead: Harvester Wheatsheaf and Atlantic Highlands, NJ: Humanities Press, 1991). Almost singlehandedly, Cooper and Mann urged the reconsideration of the whole concept of tale–teller relationships (the idea that a tale is intelligible largely or only as an expression of its teller), which had dominated Chaucerian criticism for decades. Neither is insensitive to the importance of the tellers, but together they have demonstrated, from very different vantage points, what can be gained by opening the *Canterbury Tales* to larger inquiry.

Historical Readings

A more traditional but useful study edited by Laura C. and Robert T. Lambdin, *Chaucer's Pilgrims: An Historical Guide to the Pilgrims of the Canterbury Tales* (Westport, CT and London: Praeger, 1996), provides useful historical background, as do Lillian M. Bisson, *Chaucer and the Late Medieval World* (New York: St. Martin's Press, 1998) and Henry Ansgar Kelly, *Love and Marriage in the Age of Chaucer* (Ithaca and London: Cornell University Press, 1975). On the important French influence across all of Chaucer's works, see James I. Wimsatt, *Chaucer and his French Contemporaries: Natural Music in the Fourteenth Century* (Toronto: University of Toronto Press, 1991). Other studies focus on special historical considerations, such as Norman Klassen, *Chaucer on Love, Knowledge and Sight* (Cambridge: D. S. Brewer, 1995) and Carolyn P. Collette, *Species, Phantasms, and Images: Vision and Medieval Psychology in the Canterbury Tales* (Ann Arbor: University of Michigan Press, 2001). On Chaucer's reception and reputation see now Stephanie Trigg, *Congenial Souls: Reading Chaucer from Medieval to Postmodern*, Medieval Cultures, vol. 30 (Minneapolia and London: University of Minnesota Press, 2002).

Religion

Religion is emerging (again) as a subject of much interest. Probably beginning Chaucerians should be cautioned that D. W. Robertson, Jr., *A Preface to Chaucer. Studies in Medieval Perspectives* (Princeton: Princeton University Press, 1962, reprinted 1973) is now largely discredited, as is much of the work which came from the "school" which grew up around this book, and which, with a few notable exceptions, uncritically applied a mechanical reading of Augustine, tempered by a kind of judgmental antimodernism, to Chaucer's canon. Bernard F. Huppé, *A Reading of the Canterbury Tales* (New York: State University of New York Press, 1964), is of this tradition, as is Robertson and Huppé's *Fruyt and Chaf. Studies in Chaucer's Allegories* (Princeton: Princeton University Press, 1963), though the work of John Flemming, influenced by Robertson, has given it a new focus and direction.

Among recent studies on religion, C. David Benson and Elizabeth Robertson, eds., *Chaucer's Religious Tales*, Chaucer Studies XV (Cambridge: D. S. Brewer, 1990), Roger Ellis, *Patterns of Religious Narrative in the Canterbury Tales* (London and Sydney: Croom Helm, 1986), and John M. Hill, *Chaucerian Belief. The Poetics of Reverence and Delight* (New Haven and London: Yale University Press, 1991) are particularly interesting.

Important Specialized Studies

Specialized but useful studies include: Judson Boyce Allen and Theresa Anne Moritz, *A Distinction of Stories. The Medieval Unity of Chaucer's Fair Chain of Narratives for Canterbury* (Columbus: Ohio State University Press, 1981), C. David Benson, *Chaucer's Drama of Style. Poetic Variety and Contrast in the Canterbury Tales* (Chapel Hill and London: University of North Carolina Press, 1986), John Gannon, *Chaucerian Theatricality* (Princeton: Princeton University Press, 1990), Joseph Allen Hornsby, *Chaucer and the Law* (Norman, OK: Pilgrim Books, 1988), Seth Lerer, *Chaucer and his Readers. Imagining the Author in Late-Medieval England* (Princeton: Princeton University Press, 1993), Barbara Nolan, *Chaucer and the Idea of the "Roman Antique"* (Cambridge: Cambridge University Press, 1992), J. D. North, *Chaucer's Universe* (Oxford and New York: Oxford University Press, 1988), especially good on Chaucer's astrology; Penn R. Szittya, *The Antifraternal Tradition in Medieval Literature* (Princeton: Princeton University Press, 1986), important on the exchange between the Friar and the Summoner, and on the larger issue of antifraternal satire; Mary F. Wack, *Lovesickness in the Middle Ages. The "Viaticum" and its Commentaries* (Philadelphia: University of Pennsylvania Press, 1990), especially good on the concept of love in Chaucer, including so-called "Courtly Love," on which see too N. S. Thompson, *Chaucer, Boccaccio and the Debate of Love. A Comparative Study of the* Decameron *and the* Canterbury Tales (Oxford: Clarendon Press, 1996), and James I. Wimsatt, *Chaucer and His French Contemporaries. Natural Music in the Fourteenth Century* (Toronto: University of Toronto Press, 1991). A recent collection of essays has focused on the problems posed by the *Parson's Tale*: David Raybin and Linda Tarte Holley, eds., *Closure in The Canterbury Tales. The Role of The Parson's Tale*, Studies in Medieval Culture XLI, Medieval Institute Publications (Kalamazoo: Western Michigan University, 2000). On Chaucer's use of scientific and other texts in developing the pilgrims see Walter Clyde Curry, *Chaucer and the Medieval Sciences*, second edition (New York: Barnes and Noble, 1960), originally published by Oxford University Press in 1926 – the topic is now ripe for reinvestigation. There is too a recent study by Brenda Deen Schildgen, *Pagans, Tartars, Moslems and Jews in Chaucer's* Canterbury Tales (Gainesville: University Press of Florida, 2001), which reopens the question of Chaucer's attitudes toward non-Christian attitudes and religions.

Revisionist Studies

Three recent studies read Chaucer against the cultural context within which he wrote, but from a challenging and progressive standpoint: David Aers, *Chaucer*, Harvester New Readings (Brighton: Harvester Press, 1986) and *Chaucer, Langland, and the Creative Imagination* (London: Routledge and Kegan Paul, 1980), and especially Stephen Knight, *Geoffrey Chaucer*, Rereading Literature (Oxford: Basil Blackwell, 1986). Taken together, these studies pioneered many of the now familiar concerns with culture, and helped to initiate some of the newer readings of the *Canterbury Tales*.

Index

List of Authors, Compilers, Editors, and Translators Referred to in the Select Bibliography